Series/Number 07-090

MW01033856

NONPARAMETRIC STATISTICS
An Introduction

JEAN DICKINSON GIBBONS
University of Alabama

SAGE Publications
International Educational and Professional Publisher
Newbury Park   London   New Delhi

For information address:

SAGE Publications, Inc.
2455 Teller Road
Newbury Park, California 91320
E-mail: order@sagepub.com

SAGE Publications Ltd.
6 Bonhill Street
London EC2A 4PU
United Kingdom

SAGE Publications India Pvt. Ltd.
M-32 Market
Greater Kailash I
New Delhi 110 048 India

Printed in the United States of America

Gibbons, Jean Dickinson, 1938-
    Nonparametric statistics: an introduction / Jean Dickinson Gibbons.
        p.   cm.—(Quantitative applications in the social sciences; no. 90)
    Includes bibliographical references (p.   ).
    ISBN 0-8039-3951-5 (pbk.)
    1. Nonparametric statistics. I. Title. II. Series: Sage
university papers series. Quantitative applications in the social
sciences; no. 07-090.
    QA278.8.G53   1993
    519.5—dc20
                                                            92-30724
                                                            CIP

96 97 98 99 00 01 10 9 8 7 6 5 4

Sage Production Editor: Tara S. Mead

When citing a university paper, please use the proper form. Remember to cite the current Sage University Paper series title and include the paper number. One of the following formats can be adapted (depending on the style manual used):

(1) GIBBONS, J. D. (1993) Nonparametric Statistics: An Introduction. Sage University Paper series on Quantitative Applications in the Social Sciences, 07-090. Newbury Park, CA: Sage.

OR

(2) Gibbons, J. D. (1993) *Nonparametric statistics: An introduction* (Sage University Paper series on Quantitative Applications in the Social Sciences, series no. 07-090). Newbury Park, CA: Sage.

CONTENTS

SERIES EDITOR'S INTRODUCTION

Nonparametric statistics allow hypothesis testing even when certain classical assumptions, such as interval measurement or a normal distribution, are not met. In research practice, of course, the classical assumptions are often strained. Take the case of Professor Brown, who hypothesizes that students' "interest in politics" will increase as a result of their completing Poly Sci 101. On the first and last class days, Brown administers a survey instrument with 30 ordinally scaled three-point items; for example, "I follow political news 'often,' 'sometimes,' 'never.' " (The student selects one response, scored in order 3, 2, or 1.) For each item, a difference score is created (each student's first class score is subtracted from last class score, then they are averaged). If the course has no effect, then the expectation is about 15 positive difference scores and 15 negative. However, results show 27 positive and only 3 negative. Application of a nonparametric statistic—the sign test—confirms that this lopsided finding is very unlikely and leads Brown to reject the null hypothesis.

The sign test is the simplest of the location tests discussed by Dr. Gibbons. She considers others as well, including the Mann-Whitney-Wilcoxon test (for two independent samples), the Kruskal-Wallis test (for three or more independent samples), and Friedman's test (for three or more related samples). The formal introduction of each test is followed by a data example, calculated first by hand, then by computer. The systematic presentation of relevant MINITAB and SPSSX output carries with it a critique, noting where the calculations may disagree, and why. For instance, in the solution to Example 4.1, the SPSSX and MINITAB results for the Wilcoxon rank sum test do not agree, because the former fails to include a continuity correction. Such insights as these permit the reader to give the printout calculations unusually sensitive consideration.

The data examples Dr. Gibbons provides are varied, clear, and exceptionally well chosen. They cover such topics as the effect of computer-assisted instruction, controlling the fear of vomiting, test anxiety, concept acquisition among preschoolers, measures for limited English proficiency, the ratings of U.S. presidents, and class-inclusion reasoning, to name some. Thoughtful study of these real research questions, coupled with the precise explication of each test, will soon make for proficiency in the use of this branch of distribution-free statistics. Dr. Gibbons's worthwhile monograph contributes to that expanding body of literature enabling concerned quantitative social scientists to live with (even live without) certain demanding assumptions of classical statistics.

—Michael S. Lewis-Beck
Series Editor

NONPARAMETRIC STATISTICS
An Introduction

JEAN DICKINSON GIBBONS
University of Alabama

1. INTRODUCTION

Nonparametric statistics is a collective term given to the methods of hypothesis testing and estimation that are valid under less restrictive assumptions than classical techniques. For example, the classical analysis of variance tests require the assumption of mutually independent random samples drawn from normal distributions that have equal variances, while the nonparametric counterparts require only the assumption that the samples come from any identical continuous distributions. As a result, the inference conclusions reached with nonparametric methods need not be tempered by qualifying statements as strong as, "If the distribution is normal, then . . ." . The qualifiers are always much less restrictive for nonparametric tests than for classical (or parametric) tests.

Also, classical statistical methods are strictly valid only for data measured on at least an interval scale, while nonparametric statistics apply to frequency or count data and to data measured on a nominal scale or ordinal scale. Since interval scale data can always be transformed to ranks or counts, nonparametric methods can be used whenever classical methods are valid; the reverse is not true.

Further, ordinal scale data are very frequently encountered in social and behavioral science research. Almost all opinion surveys today request answers on three-, five-, or seven-point Likert scales that measure respondents' degrees of agreement with questionnaire items. Such data are not appropriate for analysis by classical techniques because the numbers are comparable only in terms of relative magnitude, not actual magnitude. Consider a five-point Likert scale on which 1 denotes "strongly disagree," 2 denotes "disagree," 3 denotes "indifferent," 4 denotes "agree," and 5 denotes "strongly agree." A person who gives an answer of 5 agrees to a greater extent than a person giving an answer of 4, but not necessarily to the same extent as other persons

1

giving the same answer. The difference between answers 4 and 5 is not constant, as it would be for objective measurements of 4 and 5. Further, even for the same person the difference between answers 2 and 3 is not necessarily the same as the difference between answers 4 and 5. As a result, even a statistic such as the mean is not a good way to summarize Likert scale data. The median is much more appropriate because it is a positional measure. In addition, for Likert scale data the assumption of a normal distribution cannot possibly be justified. Data that come from a normal distribution can take on all real values between minus infinity and plus infinity; they are not limited to three, five, or seven integer values.

In summary, nonparametric statistics can legitimately be applied in a very wide variety of practical research situations in which classical statistics are not appropriate. The assumptions required about the population are generally quite weak, and the methods are especially appropriate for ordinal scale measurements. They are easy to use and understand.

Nonparametric methods are frequently called *distribution-free methods* because the inferences are based on a test statistic whose sampling distribution does not depend on the specific distribution of the population from which the sample is drawn.

Several statistical methods that are generally regarded as classical techniques actually are nonparametric according to these definitions. For example, methods based on the central limit theorem, Chebyshev's inequality, and many chi-square tests do not require specific distribution assumptions for large sample sizes.

Many nonparametric methods were originally proposed in the late 1940s and early 1950s. Numerous articles have appeared since then that develop properties, modifications, refinements, and extensions of the basic procedures, as well as new procedures. Considerable research is still being devoted to this topic.

This volume gives the specific methodology and logical rationale for many of the best-known and most frequently used nonparametric methods that are applicable for both small and large sample sizes. The methods are organized according to the type of sample structure that produced the data to be analyzed—for example, one sample (paired samples), two independent samples, and so forth—and the type of inference to be made (hypothesis to be tested or quantity to be estimated by a confidence interval). The inference types covered herein are limited to location tests, meaning that the null hypothesis to be tested concerns the value of a measure of central tendency, or central location, and confidence interval estimates of a measure of central tendency. The sign test and Wilcoxon signed rank test are covered in Chapter 2; Chapter 3 explains how to find corresponding confidence interval estimates of the median. The Mann-Whitney U and Wilcoxon rank sum tests, and corresponding confidence intervals for comparing the medians of two independent samples, are covered in Chapter 4. Chapters 5 and 6 extend this problem to comparing the medians of samples from three or more populations. The procedure in Chapter 5 is called the Kruskal-Wallis test; it applies when the samples are mutually independent. If the samples are related or matched, the Friedman test should be used; this is covered in Chapter 6.

There are nonparametric procedures for problems that are not related to location. We frequently want to describe the correlation, association, or agreement between two or more related groups and/or to test whether there is independence among the groups. These kinds of procedures are covered in a companion volume titled *Nonparametric Measures of Association* (Gibbons, 1992).

Each procedure described here is illustrated by one or more examples of real investigations reported in the recent social or behavioral science literature. Publication information on these journal articles appears in the reference section at the end of this volume. The necessary hand calculations are shown for these examples, and the solutions are also illustrated by computer printouts based on the MINITAB and SPSSX packages. Some limitations of these package solutions are indicated where appropriate.

An assessment of the performance of each test is also given in terms of its *asymptotic relative efficiency,* a term that is loosely defined as follows. Suppose there are two tests, A and B, either of which can be used to carry out a test of a specific null hypothesis against a specific alternative hypothesis. The asymptotic relative efficiency of test A relative to test B is the ratio of the sample size required by test B relative to the sample size required by test A in order for both tests to achieve the same power at the same significance level under the same distribution assumptions with large sample sizes. For example, suppose the asymptotic relative efficiency of a nonparametric test relative to a parametric test is computed to be 0.96 for a specific distribution. This means that the nonparametric test based on a sample of, say, 100 observations is as efficient as the corresponding parametric test based on a sample of 96 observations from this specific distribution under asymptotic theory. If the parametric test is the optimal (most powerful) test for this specific distribution, then little is lost by using the nonparametric test instead of the parametric test if the specified distribution is a reasonable assumption. But if the true distribution is not the optimal one, there may be much to gain by using the nonparametric test. The asymptotic relative efficiency would then exceed one.

Readers who are interested in more detailed information about the nonparametric methods described here should consult the books listed in Appendix B. These books also contain descriptions of other nonparametric techniques not covered in this volume.

All of the tests covered in this volume can be carried out using a computer statistical package. However, the user should be warned that almost all of the packages use the asymptotic (based on large sample theory and therefore appropriate only for large sample sizes) approximation to the sampling distribution of the test statistic in order to determine the significance or P-value. Some packages use a continuity correction and some do not. Some packages incorporate a correction for ties and some do not. As a result, hand calculations should be used if the sample size is small. If the sample size is large and a computer package is used, the manual should be read carefully to see how the test is carried out. At the present time, very few packages include confidence interval estimates based on nonparametric procedures, but MINITAB does.

2. LOCATION TESTS FOR SINGLE AND PAIRED SAMPLES (SIGN TEST AND WILCOXON SIGNED RANK TEST)

This chapter describes two nonparametric test procedures that are applicable to a single data set or data collected as pairs, such as before and after treatment. The inferences are concerned with a measure of central tendency, which is specified to be the median M of the population for the single sample case and the median M_D of the population of differences for the paired sample case, and hence these are examples of location tests. The classical counterparts of these procedures are those based on a Z statistic or a Student's t statistic, both of which require the assumption of a normal distribution.

Example 2.1

Fowler (1983) investigated the effects of computer-assisted instruction (CAI) on the ability of students to solve problems and the attitudes

TABLE 2.1
Data on Question Responses

Question	CAI	No CAI
1	.46	.41
2	.28	−.03
3	.26	−.20
4	.14	−.07
5	.64	.40
6	.35	.09
7	.62	−.01
8	.04	−.09
9	.13	.02
10	−.31	−.14
11	.15	−.02
12	−.10	−.05
13	.07	.04
14	.04	−.04
15	.46	.23
16	−.02	−.09
17	.19	.04
18	.20	−.10
19	.11	−.18
20	.18	−.18

of students toward computers and quantitative methods as problem-solving tools. The subjects, students in a management science course, were asked to respond with respect to their agreement with 20 statements on a questionnaire using a five-point Likert scale ranging from 1, "strongly disagree," to 5, "strongly agree." All statements reflected a positive attitude toward the value, usefulness, and interest in computers. Questionnaires were administered before and after students completed the course. Several sections of the course were offered; some used CAI and others did not. The data in Table 2.1 are the differences, computed as score after completing the course minus score before the course, in mean responses to the 20 questions for the students enrolled in the CAI and No CAI courses. Fowler claims that the following two research hypotheses are confirmed by these data:

1. Students exposed to CAI materials develop a more positive attitude toward computers.

2. Students not exposed to CAI materials experience no change in attitude toward computers.

We will verify these conclusions using nonparametric methods. (Fowler notes that student performance on the final examination was essentially the same for the CAI and No CAI groups, even though their attitudes were different.)

SOLUTION TO EXAMPLE 2.1: THE SIGN TEST

If there was no change in attitude toward computers for a group, the difference scores in Table 2.1 would be approximately evenly distributed around zero as positive and negative numbers. If there was an improvement in attitude, as the research hypothesis states, the number of positive scores would greatly exceed the number of negative scores. For the CAI group, there are 3 negative and 17 positive scores. For the No CAI group, there are 13 negative and 7 positive scores. These results seem intuitively to support Fowler's conclusions. We will verify them statistically by carrying out the so-called sign test on these data.

Under the null hypothesis of no change in attitude for the CAI group, the number of positive scores S follows the binomial distribution with $n = 20$ and $p = .5$. The probability of obtaining 17 or more positive scores is then calculated as

$$\Pr(S \geq 17) = \sum_{r=17}^{20} \binom{20}{r} (.5)^r (.5)^{20-r} = .0013.$$

This probability is called the exact P-value and will be used for making a decision. The number .0013 is quite small. But the 17 observed positive scores is a fact. So what can be wrong? It must be our assumption that $p = .5$, that is, that positive and negative scores have the same probability of occurrence. The data on the CAI group suggest that the probability of a positive score is greater than .5, and therefore that this group developed a more positive attitude over time.

This null hypothesis can also be tested using the normal approximation to the binomial distribution. The binomial distribution in general has mean $\mu = np$ and variance $\sigma^2 = np(1 - p)$, and these same parameters are used for the normal approximation to the binomial. The probability of 17 or more successes in 20 binomial trials is approximated by the probability that $S \geq 16.5$, where S follows the normal distribution with

$\mu = 20(.5) = 10$ and $\sigma^2 = 20(.5)(.5) = 5$. The value 16.5 is used in place of 17 to reflect a correction for continuity. This probability is

$$\Pr(S \geq 16.5) = \Pr\left(\frac{S-\mu}{\sigma} \geq \frac{16.5-10}{\sqrt{5}}\right) = \Pr(Z \geq 2.91) = .0018.$$

where the final result .0018 is read from Table A in Appendix A. Alternatively, if we specify a test at the .05 level, Table A shows that we should reject the null hypothesis if $Z \geq 1.645$. The test statistic here is $Z = 2.91$, as found above, so we reject the null hypothesis.

For the No CAI group, the research hypothesis calls for a two-sided alternative, and we observed 7 positive scores. The exact two-tailed P-value is the probability of at most 7 positive scores or at least $20 - 7 = 13$ positive scores. This is computed from the binomial distribution as

$$\sum_{r=0}^{7}\binom{20}{r}(.5)^r(.5)^{20-r} + \sum_{r=13}^{20}\binom{20}{r}(.5)^r(.5)^{20-r}$$

$$= 2\sum_{r=0}^{7}\binom{20}{r}(.5)^r(.5)^{20-r} = 2(.1316) = .2632.$$

The corresponding probability of at most 7 positive scores or at least 13 positive scores based on the normal approximation is

$$\Pr(S \leq 7.5 \text{ or } S \geq 12.5)$$

$$= \Pr\left(\frac{S-\mu}{\sigma} \leq \frac{7.5-10}{\sqrt{5}}\right) + \Pr\left(\frac{S-\mu}{\sigma} \geq \frac{12.5-10}{\sqrt{5}}\right).$$

$$= 2\Pr(Z \leq -1.12) = .2628,$$

which is quite close to the exact two-tailed P-value. This probability is not small, and therefore we accept the null hypothesis of no change in attitude by the No CAI group. The sample result could well have happened by chance.

The MINITAB solution to Example 2.1 is shown in Figure 2.1. The CAI group data are entered into c1 and the No CAI data are in c2. The first command "stest c1" and subcommand "alternative = 1" designates

8

```
MTB >   read cai into c1 and no cai into c2
DATA>   0.46 0.41
DATA>   0.28 -0.03
DATA>   0.26 -0.2
DATA>   0.14 -0.07
DATA>   0.64 0.4
DATA>   0.35 0.09
DATA>   0.62 -0.01
DATA>   0.04 -0.09
DATA>   0.13 0.02
DATA>   -0.31 -0.14
DATA>   0.15 -0.02
DATA>   -0.1 -0.05
DATA>   0.07 0.04
DATA>   0.04 -0.04
DATA>   0.46 0.23
DATA>   -0.02 -0.09
DATA>   0.19 0.04
DATA>   0.20 -0.10
DATA>   0.11 -0.18
DATA>   0.18 -0.18
     20 ROWS READ
MTB >   name c1='CAI'
MTB >   name c2='NO CAI'
MTB >   stest c1;
SUBC>   alternative=1.

SIGN TEST OF MEDIAN = 0.00000 VERSUS G.T. 0.00000

               N  BELOW  EQUAL  ABOVE  P-VALUE    MEDIAN
CAI           20      3      0     17   0.0013    0.1650
MTB >   stest c2;
SUBC>   alternative=0.

SIGN TEST OF MEDIAN = 0.00000 VERSUS N.E. 0.00000

               N  BELOW  EQUAL  ABOVE  P-VALUE    MEDIAN
NO CAI        20     13      0      7   0.2632  -0.03500
MTB >   wtest c1;
SUBC>   alternative=1.

TEST OF MEDIAN = 0.000000 VERSUS MEDIAN G.T. 0.000000

             N FOR   WILCOXON            ESTIMATED
          N  TEST   STATISTIC  P-VALUE     MEDIAN
CAI      20    20       189.0    0.001     0.1800
```

Figure 2.1. MINITAB Solution to Example 2.1

a one-tailed sign test in the positive directive for the CAI group; the exact one-tailed P-value of .0013 is given. The command "stest c2" and subcommand "alternative = 0" calls for a two-tailed sign test for the No CAI group and the exact P-value of .2632 is given. The SPSSX solution appears in Figure 2.2. Exact two-tailed P-values are given in each case.

We will now develop this test, known as the *sign test*, in general.

Assume that $X_1, X_2, \ldots, X_n$ are a random sample of n observations measured on at least an ordinal scale and drawn from a continuous population with unknown median M. We want to test a null hypothesis that specifies the value of M as M_0, or

$$H_0: M = M_0.$$

The median of a continuous population is the value that divides the area under the curve into two equal parts. Therefore, if the null hypothesis is true, M_0 is the central value and thus about one-half of the observations in the sample should be larger than M_0. The *sign test statistic* is defined as

$$S = \text{number of plus signs}$$

among the n differences $X_1 - M_0, X_2 - M_0, \ldots, X_n - M_0$. The null distribution of S is the binomial distribution with n and $p = 0.5$, or

$$\Pr(S = r) = \binom{n}{r}(.5)^r (.5)^{n-r}.$$

For sample sizes greater than 20, we can use the normal approximation to the binomial distribution with the test statistic

$$Z = \frac{S - .5n \pm .5}{\sqrt{.25n}}. \tag{2.1}$$

The $\pm .5$ term is a continuity correction introduced to improve the normal approximation to the binomial; the plus sign is used if $S < .5n$ and the minus sign is used if $S > .5n$. Any difference $X_i - M_0$ that is equal to zero is called a zero. Since the population was assumed to be continuous, zeros should occur very rarely unless the measurements are insufficiently precise. As long as there are only a few zeros, they should be ignored, and then n is reduced accordingly. Otherwise, the measurements should be made more precise.

```
data list/cai 1-5 zero 7
npar tests sign=cai with  zero
begin data
0.46    0
0.28    0
0.26    0
0.14    0
0.64    0
0.35    0
0.62    0
0.04    0
0.13    0
-0.31   0
0.15    0
-0.1    0
0.07    0
0.04    0
0.46    0
-0.02   0
0.19    0
0.2     0
0.11    0
0.18    0
end data
```

```
- - - - -  Sign Test
        CAI
with ZERO

          Cases

            17  -  Diffs (ZERO LT CAI)
             3  +  Diffs (ZERO GT CAI)   (Binomial)
             0     Ties                  2-Tailed P = .0026
            __
            20     Total
```

Figure 2.2. SPSSX Solution to Example 2.1 (page 1 of 3)

The alternative to H_0 is called the research (or alternative) hypothesis and is denoted by A. Suppose A is one-sided in the positive direction as

$$A_+: M > M_0.$$

```
data list/nocai 1-6 zero 8
npar tests sign=nocai with zero
begin data
0.41    0
-0.03   0
-0.2    0
-0.07   0
0.4     0
0.09    0
-0.01   0
-0.09   0
0.02    0
-0.14   0
-0.02   0
-0.05   0
0.04    0
-0.04   0
0.23    0
-0.09   0
0.04    0
-0.1    0
-0.18   0
-0.18   0
end data
```

- - - - - Sign Test
    NOCAI
with ZERO

          Cases

          7   -   Diffs (ZERO LT NOCAI)
          13   +   Diffs (ZERO GT NOCAI) (Binomial)
          0   Ties   2-Tailed P = .2632
          ──
          20   Total

Figure 2.2. SPSSX Solution to Example 2.1 (page 2 of 3)

If A_+ is true, the number of sample observations larger than M_0 will be large and therefore S will be large. As a result, with the alternative A_+ the appropriate rejection region for the test statistic S or Z is large values, that is, in the right tail of the sampling distribution of S or Z. Similarly, if the alternative is one-sided in the negative direction as

```
data list/cai 1-5 zero 7
npar tests wilcoxon = all
begin data
0.46   0
0.28   0
0.26   0
0.14   0
0.64   0
0.35   0
0.62   0
0.04   0
0.13   0
-0.31  0
0.15   0
-0.1   0
0.07   0
0.04   9
0.46   0
-0.02  0
0.19   0
0.2    0
0.11   0
0.18   0
end data
```

```
- - - - -   Wilcoxon Matched-Pairs Signed-Ranks Test
        CAI
with ZERO

        Mean Rank    Cases

            11.12        17   -   Ranks  (ZERO LT CAI)
             7.00         3   +   Ranks  (ZERO GT CAI)
                          0       Ties   (ZERO EQ CAI)
                         ──
                         20       Total
     Z = -3.1359                    2-Tailed P = .0017
```

Figure 2.2. SPSSX Solution to Example 2.1 (page 3 of 3)

$$A_-: M < M_0,$$

the appropriate rejection region for S or Z is small values, that is, in the left tail of the sampling distribution of S or Z.

The conclusion in nonparametric testing is frequently given in terms of P-values. In general, the P-value for an observed value of the test statistic is the probability under H_0 of obtaining a sample result as extreme as that observed in a particular direction as indicated by the one-sided alternative. In Example 2.1 the alternative for the CAI group is in the positive direction; therefore, the appropriate direction for the P-value is large values of S. Since we found $S = 17$, the appropriate P-value is $\Pr(S \geq 17) = .0013$. If we want to use this P-value to reach a decision at $\alpha = .05$, say, we reject H_0 in favor of A_+ because $P < \alpha$. If the alternative is one-sided in the negative direction, the appropriate P-value is in the left tail of the sampling distribution. If the alternative is two-sided as

$$A: M \neq M_0,$$

the common practice is to report twice the smaller one-tailed P-value, or one, whichever is smaller.

In general, the decision rule using P-values is to reject H_0 for any $P \leq \alpha$ and not to reject otherwise. Alternatively, we can choose simply to report the P-value and not select a particular value of α.

For the sign test the appropriate P-values for the test statistic S are in the right tail for the alternative A_+, left tail for A_-, and twice the smaller tail probability for A; for larger sample sizes the same tail probabilities are used for the test statistic Z in Equation 2.1.

While exact P-values for the sign test statistic can always be calculated from the binomial distribution, they can also be easily read from Table B, Appendix A, for $n \leq 20$. For a given n, the entry in the column labeled P is the left-tail cumulative probability for the corresponding number in the column labeled Left S, and this same value is the right-tail probability for the corresponding number in the column labeled Right S. For example, with $n = 10$, $\Pr(S \leq 2) = \Pr(S \geq 8) = .0547$. Thus this table makes use of the fact that for any sample size n, the distribution of S under H_0 is symmetric about $n/2$.

For paired sample data, $(X_1, Y_1), (X_2, Y_2), \ldots, (X_n, Y_n)$, the same procedure can be used to test the null hypothesis

$$H_0: M_D = M_0,$$

where M_D represents the median of the population of differences $X - Y$. In this kind of application, S is defined as the number of plus signs among the n differences $X_1 - Y_1 - M_0, X_2 - Y_2 - M_0, \ldots, X_n - Y_n - M_0$. The data in Example 2.1 actually represented paired samples, because the numbers given in Table 2.1 were the differences in scores on each question, after minus before, so no further differences needed to be taken. If, however, we wanted to compare the CAI group with the No CAI group, we would use the sign test on the differences of the paired observations in Table 2.1. This will be left as an exercise for the reader.

ALTERNATIVE SOLUTION TO EXAMPLE 2.1: WILCOXON SIGNED RANK TEST

We use the data in Example 2.1 to illustrate a different nonparametric method of analyzing the data on scores, after completing the course minus before completing the course, for the group that took the CAI course. The sign test used only the information about signs of the data on scores, and not the information about relative magnitudes. Here we have to assume that the scores are symmetric about the median M and formulate the null hypothesis that $M = 0$. In this case we expect not only the same number of positive and negative scores but also that the magnitudes of the positive and negative scores will balance out. To measure this in the sample data, we take the absolute values of the scores and rank them from 1 to 20, keeping track of the original signs. This is done in Table 2.2 for the CAI group. Observations having the same absolute value (called tied) are each given the same rank, called the midrank and defined as the mean of the ranks they would have been given if they had not been tied.

Under the null hypothesis here, we expect the sum T_+ of the ranks of observations that were originally positive to be about equal to the corresponding sum T_- of the ranks for the negative observations. Here $T_+ = 189$ and $T_- = 21$, a wide divergence in values. We test the significance of this result using the normal approximation to the distribution of T_+ and obtain a P-value of .0009. This probability is very small, and therefore we conclude that the median M is larger than zero, and equivalently that the CAI group experienced an improved attitude toward computers after taking the course.

The last part of the MINITAB printout solution to Example 2.1 shows the command "wtest c1" and subcommand "alternative = 1." This calls for the Wilcoxon signed rank statistic calculated for the CAI group with a one-tailed test in the positive direction. The value of the test statistic $T_+ = 189$ is shown with the one-tailed P-value of .001, based on the

TABLE 2.2
Calculations Based on Table 2.1 Data

Question	Sign	$|CA|$	Rank
1	+	.46	17.5
2	+	.28	14
3	+	.26	13
4	+	.14	8
5	+	.64	20
6	+	.35	16
7	+	.62	19
8	+	.04	2.5
9	+	.13	7
10	−	.31	15
11	+	.15	9
12	−	.10	5
13	+	.07	4
14	+	.04	2.5
15	+	.46	17.5
16	−	.02	1
17	+	.19	11
18	+	.20	12
19	+	.11	6
20	+	.18	10

normal approximation with a continuity correction; this result agrees with ours. The last part of the SPSSX solution to Example 2.1 gives the mean rank of 11.12 for 17 cases, which translates to $T_+ = 17(11.12) = 189$. The two-tailed P-value based on the normal approximation is not the same as ours because SPSSX does not use a continuity correction.

Now we generalize the test used in this alternative solution to Example 2.1 for a random sample $X_1, X_2, \ldots, X_n$ measured on at least an ordinal scale and drawn from a continuous population that is assumed to be a symmetric distribution. For any symmetric distribution, the mean and median are equal. Our null hypothesis specifies a value M_0 for the median of this symmetric distribution. If the null hypothesis H_0: $M = M_0$ is true, then we expect not only that about one-half of the sample observations will exceed M_0 but also that the magnitudes of those observations that are larger than M_0 will about balance off the magnitudes of those smaller than M_0, because the distribution is symmetric about M_0 under H_0. The appropriate procedure here, then, is to rank the absolute values $|X_1 - M_0|, |X_2 - M_0|, \ldots, |X_n - M_0|$ from 1 to n, keeping track of the original signs. Those ranks that are from originally positive differences $X_i - M_0$ are called positive ranks and those ranks from originally negative differences are called negative ranks. The sum of the positive ranks should be about equal to the sum of the negative ranks if H_0 is true. However, since these two sums add up to a constant, $1 + 2 + \ldots + n = n(n + 1)/2$, either one can be used as a test statistic by itself. The *Wilcoxon signed rank test statistic* is defined as either

$$T_+ = \text{sum of positive ranks, or}$$

$$T_- = \text{sum of negative ranks.}$$

Note that T_- is always positive, given that it is a sum of ranks, which are always positive. The test statistics T_+ and T_- are identically distributed under the null hypothesis. This distribution is given here for $n \leq 15$ as Table C, Appendix A, where T is to be interpreted as either T_+ or T_-.

If the alternative A_+: $M > M_0$ is true, T_+ should be much larger than its expected value under H_0, and therefore the appropriate P-value is in the right tail for T_+. We obtain the same P-value if we use a left-tail probability for T_-. For the alternative A_- : $M < M_0$, the appropriate P-value is either in the left tail for T_+ or in the right tail for T_-. With a two-sided alternative A: $M \neq M_0$, the appropriate P-value is twice the right-tail probability for the larger of T_+ or T_-.

The exact tail probabilities given in Table C for the Wilcoxon signed rank test statistic make use of the fact that T is symmetrically distributed about its mean $n(n + 1)/4$. Thus the notation here is exactly the same as for Table B, Appendix A, in that for a given n the entry in the column labeled P is a left-tail probability for the entry in the column labeled Left T and this same value is also a right-tail probability for the corresponding entry in the column labeled Right T, where T is interpreted as either T_+ or T_-. Thus for $n = 10$, $\Pr(T \leq 9) = \Pr(T \geq 46) = .032$.

With a small sample size it is easy to see how the entries in Table C were obtained. Consider the case where $n = 3$. We know that the ranks must be 1, 2, and 3, and so the only issue is which ranks are positive ranks and which ranks are negative ranks. There are $2^3 = 8$ different ways of associating signs with these three ranks, and each different way is equally likely under the null hypothesis; hence each has probability $1/8$. To calculate the sampling distribution of, say, T_+, we simply enumerate the eight possible assignments of signs, calculate T_+ for each,

TABLE 2.3
Possible Assignments of Signs

Positive Ranks	Negative Ranks	Value of T_+	Probability
None	1, 2, 3	0	1/8
1	2, 3	1	1/8
2	1, 3	2	1/8
3	1, 2	3	1/8
1, 2	3	3	1/8
1, 3	2	4	1/8
2, 3	1	5	1/8
1, 2, 3	None	6	1/8

and cumulate the resulting probabilities as shown in Table 2.3. From Table 2.3 we see that $\Pr(T_+ \le 2) = 3/8$ and $\Pr(T_+ \le 3) = 5/8$, which agree with the corresponding entries in Table C.

The null distribution of T approaches the normal distribution, and this approximation is reasonably accurate for $n \ge 16$. The test statistics corresponding to T_+ and T_- (with a continuity correction) are

$$Z_{+,R} = \frac{T_+ - .5 - n(n+1)/4}{\sqrt{n(n+1)(2n+1)/24}} \qquad Z_{-,R} = \frac{T_- - .5 - n(n+1)/4}{\sqrt{n(n+1)(2n+1)/24}}. \quad (2.2)$$

The sum of all the ranks is $1 + 2 + \ldots + n = n(n+1)/2$, and hence the mean of both T_+ and T_- is one-half of this sum or $n(n+1)/4$. The expression in the denominators of Equation 2.2 is the standard deviation of T_+ and T_-. The appropriate P-values are in the right tail for $Z_{+,R}$ with the alternative A_+, right tail for $Z_{-,R}$ with A_-, and twice the right-tail probability for the larger of $Z_{+,R}$ and $Z_{-,R}$ with A. All of these tail probabilities are found from Table A, Appendix A.

Two problems that can arise in applications are zeros and ties. Because a zero is neither positive nor negative, each zero should be ignored, and n is reduced accordingly. A tie occurs whenever two or more absolute values of differences are equal—for example, $|X_i - M_0| = |X_j - M_0|$—for some i and j. Ties should not be discarded. The accepted procedure is to assign each absolute difference in any tied set the midrank, defined as the average of the ranks they would be assigned if they were not tied. Zeros and ties should not be extensive when the assumption of a continuous distribution is met. In this case, the tests can be used in exactly the same way to give approximate P-values. If the zeros and/or ties are extensive, more precise measurement techniques should be used. Many books give formulas like Equation 2.2 that include a correction for ties for this and most other tests covered in this monograph. These adjustments are not given here because they add to the difficulty of computation and seldom affect the conclusion. Since most computer packages calculate test statistics both with and without the correction for ties, the researcher should examine both before reaching a conclusion.

The Wilcoxon signed rank test can be used in exactly the same way for paired sample data, (X_1, Y_1), (X_2, Y_2), . . . , (X_n, Y_n). The null hypothesis here is $H_0: M_D = M_0$, where M_D is the median of the population of differences $D = X - Y$. The signed rank statistic is calculated in the same way as before, but by assigning ranks to the absolute values $|X_i - Y_i - M_0|$.

Notice that since the Wilcoxon signed rank test assumes a symmetric distribution of X (and D for paired samples) and the mean μ and median M are always equal for symmetric distributions, the null hypothesis could have been written in terms of μ (or μ_D).

Example 2.2

Philips (1985) has reported on an experiment in which seven patients (five females and two males) with a fear of vomiting were given group exposure treatment sessions involving repeated exposures to a four-minute film portraying scenes of men and women vomiting. The anticipated effect of these exposures was a reduction of anxiety about vomiting and feelings of nausea. Each patient was given a Fear of Negative Evaluation (FNE) score before and after the treatment sessions. These scores are shown in Table 2.4 (larger numbers indicate greater fear). Did the treatment sessions have the anticipated effect?

SOLUTION TO EXAMPLE 2.2:
WILCOXON SIGNED RANK TEST

Let D denote the before minus after $(X - Y)$ FNE score. The appropriate hypothesis set is

$$H_0: M_D = 0 \qquad A_+: M_D > 0,$$

given that the researchers anticipated reduced FNE scores after treatment.

TABLE 2.4
Data on FNE Scores

Patient	Before (X)	After (Y)
1	10.60	7.15
2	7.90	9.36
3	12.40	6.27
4	16.80	7.19
5	13.20	5.45
6	14.70	6.21
7	18.34	8.00

We will assume that the distribution of differences is symmetric and carry out the Wilcoxon signed rank test. Table 2.5 shows the differences D, their absolute values $|D|$, and the ranks of $|D|$. The computed values of the test statistics are $T_+ = 27$, $T_- = 1$, and the corresponding one-tailed P-value is .016 from Table C, Appendix A. With such a small P-value, we conclude that there is sufficient evidence that the treatment sessions were effective in reducing scores on the Fear of Negative Evaluation test.

The two computer printouts presented in Figures 2.3 and 2.4 show the MINITAB and SPSSX solutions to Example 2.2. For MINITAB the X data are entered into c1 and the Y data into c2; the instruction is to take the differences $X - Y$ and enter them into c3; the next command and subcommand call for a one-tailed Wilcoxon signed rank test for the data in c3 in the positive direction. The Wilcoxon statistic $T_+ = 27$ agrees with ours, but the P-value .017 is based on the normal approximation with a continuity correction. This approximation is surprisingly close for such a small sample size.

TABLE 2.5
Calculations for Wilcoxon Signed Rank Test

Patient	X	Y	D	|D|	Rank|D|	Sign D
1	10.60	7.15	3.45	3.45	2	+
2	7.90	9.36	-1.46	1.46	1	-
3	12.40	6.27	6.13	6.13	3	+
4	16.80	7.19	9.61	9.61	6	+
5	13.20	5.45	7.75	7.75	4	+
6	14.70	6.21	8.49	8.49	5	+
7	18.34	8.00	10.34	10.34	7	+

```
MTB >    set X Before into c1
DATA>    10.6 7.90 12.40 16.80 13.20 14.70 18.34
MTB >    set Y After into c2
DATA>    7.15 9.36 6.27 7.19 5.45 6.21 8.00
MTB >    let c3=c1-c2
MTB >    name c3='X-Y'
MTB >    print c3


X-Y
   3.45  -1.46  6.13    9.61    7.75    8.49    10.34


MTB >    wtest c3;
SUBC>    alternative=1.

TEST OF MEDIAN = 0.000000 VERSUS MEDIAN G.T.  0.000000

                  N FOR    WILCOXON                ESTIMATED
          N       TEST    STATISTIC  P-VALUE        MEDIAN
X-Y       7        7         27.0     0.017          6.917
```

Figure 2.3. MINITAB Solution to Example 2.2

The SPSSX solution shows a mean value of 4.5, which represents our $T_+ = 27$ divided by 6, the number of positive ranks among the $X - Y$ differences. The solution uses the normal approximation without a continuity correction to obtain an approximate one-tailed P-value of .0280/2 = .014. This approximation should not be used because it is not accurate with a sample size as small as 7.

Whenever sample data are measurements, as in Examples 2.1 and 2.2, either the sign test or the Wilcoxon signed rank test can be used. The distribution of measurements must be assumed to be symmetric if the signed rank test is to be applied, but this assumption is not needed for use of the sign test. In general, if either test can be applied, the Wilcoxon signed rank test is preferred if the symmetry assumption appears reasonable, because it makes use of more of the available information.

The next example illustrates a situation in which only the sign test is appropriate, because the data are not measurements.

Example 2.3

Covington and Omelich (1987) report on a study to investigate the research hypothesis that anxiety tends to inhibit academic performance

```
data list/before 1-5 after 7-11
npar tcsts wilcoxon = all
begin data
10.60 7.15
 7.90 9.36
12.40 6.27
16.80 7.19
13.20 5.45
14.70 6.21
18.34 8.00
end data
```

```
- - - - Wilcoxon Matched-Pairs Signed-Ranks Test
    BEFORE
with AFTER

    Mean Rank  Cases

        4.50  6 - Ranks (AFTER LT BEFORE)
        1.00  1 + Ranks (AFTER GT BEFORE)
              0   Ties  (AFTER EQ BEFORE)
              ─
              7   Total
        Z = - 2.1974     2-Tailed P = .0280
```

Figure 2.4. SPSSX Solution to Example 2.2

by temporarily blocking previously learned responses, especially on written tests. Students in an introductory psychology class at the University of California at Berkeley were given the 40-item Reactions to Test (RTT) instrument to classify them into two groups according to high and low test anxiety. During the semester, the students were regularly given 12-item multiple-choice quizzes consisting of 6 difficult questions and 6 easy questions. A preliminary test was carried out to show that all students could easily distinguish between the difficult and the easy questions. To investigate the research hypothesis, the researchers gave a random sample of students in the high-anxiety group a usual 12-item quiz. The next day, the same students were given a quiz with the exact same questions, but with the order of the questions changed. This exercise had not been previously announced, and it occurred before the students were given feedback on their performance on the previous day. The researchers reduced anxiety levels for this

TABLE 2.6
Scores on Tests

Student	Test 1	Test 2
1	0	0
2	0	0
3	0	0
4	0	1
5	1	1
6	1	1
7	1	2
8	1	2
9	1	2
10	1	2
11	2	2
12	2	2
13	2	3
14	2	3
15	3	3
16	3	4
17	4	4
18	4	5
19	4	5
20	4	5

second quiz by informing the students that it was for experimental purposes only, that the outcome would not affect their course grades, and that there was no time limit. The students were told to give the answers they considered correct even if they differed from their answers on the previous day's test. Changes in test performance were measured by noting the number of correct answers for the 6 difficult questions only, hence the only possible scores are 0, 1, . . . , 6. Simulated data for 20 students are shown in Table 2.6. Do these data support the research hypothesis?

SOLUTION TO EXAMPLE 2.3: THE SIGN TEST

Let D denote the Test 2 score minus the Test 1 score. The research hypothesis states that the median of D should be larger than zero, so the hypothesis set is

$$H_0: M_D \leq 0 \qquad A_+: M_D > 0.$$

```
MTB > read test one into c1 and test two into c2
DATA> 0 0
DATA> 0 0
DATA> 0 0
DATA> 0 1
DATA> 1 1
DATA> 1 1
DATA> 1 2
DATA> 1 2
DATA> 1 2
DATA> 1 2
DATA> 2 2
DATA> 2 2
DATA> 2 3
DATA> 2 3
DATA> 3 3
DATA> 3 4
DATA> 4 4
DATA> 4 5
DATA> 4 5
DATA> 4 5
DATA> end
  20 ROWS READ
MTB > let c3=c2-c1
MTB > name c3='t2-t1'
MTB > print c3

t2-t1
  0   0   0   1   0   0   1   1   1   1   0   0   1   1   0
  1   0   1   1   1

MTB > stest c3;
SUBC> alternative=1.

SIGN TEST OF MEDIAN = 0.00000 VERSUS G.T. 0.00000

              N  BELOW  EQUAL  ABOVE  P-VALUE   MEDIAN
t2-t1        20     0      9     11   0.0005    1.000

MTB > sinterval 95 c3

SIGN CONFIDENCE INTERVAL FOR MEDIAN

                      ACHIEVED
         N  MEDIAN  CONFIDENCE  CONFIDENCE INTERVAL  POSITION
t2-t1   20   1.000     0.8847  ( 0.000, 1.000 )         7
                       0.9500  ( 0.000, 1.000 )       NLI
                       0.9586  ( 0.000, 1.000 )         6
```

Figure 2.5. MINITAB Solution to Example 2.3

```
data list /test1 1 test2 3
npar tests sign = test2 with test1
begin data
0 0
0 0
0 0
0 1
1 1
1 1
1 2
1 2
1 2
1 2
2 2
2 2
2 3
2 3
3 3
3 4
4 4
4 5
4 5
4 5
end data
```

```
- - - - -  Sign Test
     TEST2
with TEST1

          Cases

          11  - Diffs (TESTI LT TEST2)
           0  + Diffs (TESTI GT TEST2)  (Binomial)
           9    Ties                    2-Tailed P = .0010
          ──
          20    Total
```

Figure 2.6. SPSSX Solution to Example 2.3

The sample differences are all either 0 or +1; hence the measurement scale is too unrefined to note anything other than the signs. The number of plus signs is $S = 11$. The one-tailed P-value is .0005 for $n = 11$ (reduced for the nine zeros) from Table B, Appendix A, and hence the data support the research hypothesis. The MINITAB and SPSSX solutions to Example 2.3 appear in Figures 2.5 and 2.6. The results agree exactly with ours.

Both the sign test and the Wilcoxon signed rank test are nonparametric alternatives to the Student's t test for one sample or paired samples. The Student's t test requires the assumption of a normal distribution, for which the mean and median are equal. The asymptotic relative efficiency of the sign test relative to the Student's t test is .67 for normal distributions and is at least .33 for any continuous symmetric distribution. The asymptotic relative efficiency of the sign test is larger than 1.00 for some distributions.

The asymptotic relative efficiency of the Wilcoxon signed rank test relative to Student's t test is .955 for normal distributions, 1.00 for the continuous uniform distribution, at least .864 for any continuous symmetric distribution, and generally larger than 1.00 for distributions whose tails are longer than those of a normal distribution. Therefore, if the assumption of a symmetric distribution appears reasonable, little efficiency is lost using the nonparametric Wilcoxon signed rank test, which does not require the assumption of a normal distribution, and considerable efficiency may be gained. Recall that there are many distributions other than a normal one that are symmetric, such as a rectangular or uniform distribution, triangular distribution, and U-shaped distribution.

3. CONFIDENCE INTERVAL ESTIMATES OF THE MEDIAN AND MEDIAN DIFFERENCE FOR SINGLE AND PAIRED SAMPLES

The sign test and Wilcoxon signed rank procedures for testing hypotheses about the value of the median M (or median difference M_D) have corresponding procedures to establish confidence interval estimates of M (or M_D). This chapter explains how those confidence intervals are obtained.

In general, a 95% confidence interval for M corresponds to a two-sided test of H_0: $M = M_0$ versus A: $M \neq M_0$ at the .05 level in the following way. The 95% confidence interval consists of all those values of M_0 in H_0 that would lead to acceptance of H_0 at significance level 1 − .95 = .05, the complement of the level of confidence. Thus the confidence interval endpoints represent the most extreme values of M_0 that would lead to acceptance of H_0.

The confidence interval for the median corresponding to the one-sample sign test has endpoints that are order statistics of the sample. For a sample of size n containing observations $X_1, X_2, \ldots, X_n$, the order statistics are simply the sample data (the same numerical values) rearranged in order of relative magnitude, that is, in an ordered array, denoted by $X_{(1)}$, $X_{(2)}, \ldots, X_{(n)}$. Thus $X_{(k)}$ is the kth from the smallest among $X_1, X_2, \ldots$, X_n, and X_{n-k+1} is the $(n - k + 1)$th from the smallest, which is equivalent to the kth from the largest in the arrayed data. Since the confidence interval estimate should be symmetric about the sample median, the endpoints will be the kth from the smallest and the kth from the largest data values, or

$$X_{(k)} \le M \le X_{(n-k+1)}. \tag{3.1}$$

If the data are pairs (X, Y), the endpoints are the kth from the smallest and kth from the largest among the n differences $(X - Y)$, and the confidence interval estimates the value of the median difference M_D. As a result, we need only state the required value of k in order to find numerical values for the endpoints in any data set.

For sample sizes greater than 20, the value of k in Equation 3.1 based on the normal approximation to the binomial distribution is

$$k = .5(n + 1 - Z_{\alpha/2}\sqrt{n}), \tag{3.2}$$

where $Z_{\alpha/2}$ is the value from Table A, Appendix A, that corresponds to a right-tail probability of $Z_{\alpha/2}$ for a confidence coefficient equal to $1 - \alpha$. Thus if we want a 95% confidence interval we use $Z_{.025} = 1.96$ in Equation 3.2. If $n = 25$ and the confidence level is 90%, $Z_{.05} = 1.645$ and substitution in Equation 3.2 gives

$$k = .5(26 - 1.645 \sqrt{25}) = 8.89.$$

As we can see, k as calculated from Equation 3.2 is generally not an integer, and it must be for practical use. The conservative approach is to round the numerical result down to the next smaller integer. For $n = 25$ and 90% confidence, the endpoints are the eighth from the smallest and the eighth from the largest observations in the array, that is, the observed values $X_{(8)}$ and $X_{(18)}$.

For small sample sizes we must use Table B, Appendix A, to find the value of k. Because the binomial distribution is discrete, the range of possible confidence levels is also discrete. The only possible exact confidence coefficients for given n are $1 - 2P$, where P is an entry in Table B for that value of n. For example, with $n = 10$ and confidence near .90, say, one choice for exact confidence level is $1 - 2(.0547) = .8906$. Note that this .8906 level corresponds to a left-tail P-value of .0547, which holds for $S \leq 2$; the number 2 in the column headed Left S is the third from the smallest for $n = 10$. Hence $k = 3$ for confidence level .8906. Similarly, with $n = 10$ we would use $k = 2$ for confidence coefficient $1 - 2(.0107) = .9896$.

In general, for small sample sizes, the first step is to choose an exact confidence level $1 - 2P$ that corresponds to an entry P in Table B for the given sample size n (not reduced for zeros). Then the value of k to use in Equation 3.1 is the rank of the corresponding entry in the column labeled Left S for that n.

Example 3.1

The procedure for finding a confidence interval for the median based on the sign test procedure will be illustrated with the No CAI group data given in Table 2.1 with $n = 20$ observations. Table B shows that our choices for confidence levels are $1 - 2(.0557) = .8846$ with $k = 7$ and $1 - 2(.0207) = .9586$ with $k = 6$. We will choose the latter, so we need to determine the sixth from the smallest and sixth from the largest observations. The array of all 20 observations is as follows:

$$-.20, -.18, -.18, -.14, -.10, -.09, -.09, -.07, -.05, -.04, -.03, -.02,$$
$$-.01, .02, .04, .04, .09, .23, .40, .41.$$

The sixth smallest and largest are $-.09$ and $.04$, respectively, and therefore the confidence interval estimate is

$$-.09 \leq M \leq .04,$$

with confidence coefficient .9586. Note that the value zero is included in this confidence interval. This means that the test of H_0: $M = 0$ versus A: $M \neq 0$ at significance level $1 - .9586 = .0414$ would not lead to rejection.

The MINITAB solution to Example 3.1 is shown in Figure 3.1. The command "sinterval 95" means that the sign test confidence interval is to have confidence near .95. The solution gives the two exact intervals with confidence .8847 and .9586 (the latter agrees with ours), which are the only two attainable confidence levels that bracket .95. The interval with confidence labeled .95 is based on the normal approximation to

28

```
MTB >  set no cai in c1
DATA> 0.41 -0.03 -0.2 -0.07 0.4 0.09 -0.01 -0.09 0.02 -0.14
-0.02 -0.05 0.04
DATA>  -0.04 0.23 -0.09 0.04 -0.1 -0.18 -0.18
DATA>  end    7.15 9.36 6.27 7.19 5.45 6.21 8.00
MTB >  name c1='no cai'
MTB >  sinterval 95 c1

SIGN CONFIDENCE INTERVAL FOR MEDIAN

                      ACHIEVED
       N    MEDIAN   CONFIDENCE CONFIDENCE INTERVAL   POSITION
no cai 20  -0.03500   0.8847   (-0.09000, 0.02000)        7
                      0.9500   (-0.09000, 0.03530)      NLI
                      0.9586   (-0.09000, 0.04000)        6
```

Figure 3.1. MINITAB Solution to Example 3.1

the value of k and the upper endpoint is a (nonlinear) interpolated value between .02 and .04. Interpolation was not necessary for the lower limit because the sixth- and seventh-smallest order statistics are tied. With 20 observations the normal approximation is sufficiently accurate.

The confidence interval estimate of the median based on the Wilcoxon signed rank test procedure and assuming symmetry is found in a similar manner. The confidence interval endpoints are the kth from the smallest and kth from the largest among the $n(n + 1)/2$ Walsh averages for a sample $X_1, X_2, \ldots, X_n$. The *Walsh averages* are defined as the averages of each observation with every other observation, including itself, that is $(X_i + X_j)/2$ for all $i, j = 1, 2, \ldots, n$. In general, there are a total of $n(n + 1)/2$ Walsh averages. For large sample sizes the value of k for confidence level $1 - \alpha$ is

$$k = .5 + n(n + 1)/4 - Z_{\alpha/2}\sqrt{n(n + 1)(2n + 1)/24},\qquad (3.3)$$

which is rounded down to the next smaller integer. For small sample sizes the value of k is found from Table C, Appendix A, for confidence level $1 - 2P$, where P is an entry for the sample size n. Once P is located, the value of k equals the rank of the corresponding entry in the column headed Left T for that n. For example, with $n = 10$, $P = .024$, we find $k = 9$ for confidence level $1 - 2(.024) = .952$. The confidence interval endpoints are the ninth smallest and ninth largest of the $10(11)/2 = 55$

TABLE 3.1
Calculation of Walsh Averages

−1.46	3.45	6.13	7.75	8.49	9.61	10.34
0.995	4.79	6.94	8.12	9.05	9.975	
2.335	5.60	7.31	8.68	9.415		
3.145	5.97	7.87	9.045			
3.515	6.53	8.235				
4.075	6.895					
4.44						

Walsh averages. Note that all zeros are counted and all ties are counted as many times as they appear among these Walsh averages.

If the data are paired, the Walsh averages are computed from the differences $D = X - Y$, as shown in Example 3.2.

Example 3.2

This confidence interval procedure is illustrated for the $n = 7$ paired data points on FNE scores given earlier in Table 2.4. Note that with confidence interval estimation we pay no attention to the research hypothesis because there is no null hypothesis. For $n = 7$, Table C, Appendix A, shows that a reasonable confidence level would be $1 - 2(.039) = .922$, which corresponds to a Left T of 3 with rank $k = 4$. The $7(8)/2 = 28$ Walsh averages of the differences D (not $|D|$) from Table 2.5 are given in Table 3.1.

Note that the differences D are arranged in an array to form the first row of Table 3.1. These represent the Walsh averages of each observation with itself. The first column is then completed by averaging the smallest observation −1.46 with every other observation in the first row. The second column is completed by averaging 3.45 with every other observation to its right, and so on. This makes the numbers in each column appear in an ordered array, and also the numbers in each row. This ordering makes it easy to see that the fourth-smallest and fourth-largest values in Table 3.1 are 3.145 and 9.415, respectively, and our confidence interval estimate is $3.145 \leq M_D \leq 9.415$ with 92.2% confidence. The MINITAB solution to Example 3.2 shown in Figure 3.2 uses the command "winterval 92.2" to obtain an interval based on the normal approximation with confidence coefficient estimated by .924.

```
MTB >    set X Before into c1
DATA>    10.6 7.90 12.40 16.80 13.20 14.70 18.34
MTB >    set Y After into c2
DATA>    7.15 9.36 6.27 7.19 5.45 6.21 8.00
MTB >    let c3=c1-c2
MTB >    name c3='X-Y'
MTB >    print c3

X-Y
    3.45    -1.46   6.13    9.61    7.75    8.49    10.34

MTB >           winterval 92.2 c3

                ESTIMATED   ACHIEVED
                N   MEDIAN  CONFIDENCE CONFIDENCE INTERVAL
X-Y             7   6.92        92.4 (    3.14,    9.41)
```

Figure 3.2. MINITAB Solution to Example 3.2

In finding a confidence interval estimate of the median or median difference by either of these procedures, zeros in the original data or zeros in the differences are not excluded, and therefore the sample size n is not reduced. But these zeros are eliminated in hypothesis testing, and then n must be reduced. As a result, if there are many zeros, more power will be obtained if the hypothesis-testing problem is approached by finding the corresponding confidence interval. In Example 2.3, we had nine zeros with a sample of size 20, hence a confidence interval solution to this example would have been better. The MINITAB solution to Example 2.3 given in Figure 2.5 shows that the confidence interval using all 20 observations and the normal approximation is $0 \leq M_D \leq 1$, which leads to the conclusion that the data do not support the research hypothesis.

4. LOCATION TESTS AND CONFIDENCE INTERVALS FOR TWO INDEPENDENT SAMPLES (MANN-WHITNEY-WILCOXON TEST)

This chapter illustrates a nonparametric test and confidence interval procedure for comparing the central tendency of two independent random samples. These methods require only the assumption of continuous distributions and are nonparametric alternatives to the classical Student's

t test or ANOVA test that requires the assumption of normal distributions with equal variances. We start with a numerical example.

Example 4.1

Williams and Carnine (1981) compared two different methods of training preschool children to understand an unfamiliar concept. The unfamiliar concept was called a "Gerbie," defined as a line angle between 0 and 110 degrees from the horizontal plane. Fourteen children were divided randomly into two groups of seven each, an experimental group and a control group. Children in the experimental group were shown 8 positive and 4 negative examples of a Gerbie and told in each case whether the example was positive or negative. Children in the control group were shown 12 positive examples. To determine how well the children learned the concept, 18 new examples, 9 positive and 9 negative, were later shown to each child. Suppose the scores shown below are the number of correct identifications among these 18. Determine whether the experimental group represents a population with a larger median score than that of the control group at the .05 level.

experimental: 15, 18, 8, 15, 17, 16, 13

control: 10, 5, 4, 9, 12, 6, 7

SOLUTION TO EXAMPLE 4.1:
MANN-WHITNEY-WILCOXON TEST

The scores of the experimental and control groups represent two mutually independent random samples. If the experimental group has a larger median score M_E than the control group median M_C in general, most of the experimental sample scores E will be larger than most of the control sample scores C. To see if this is true, we pool the 14 scores into a single ordered array, keeping track of which sample produced which score by underlining the experimental scores. The array is as follows:

4, 5, 6, 7, 8, 9, 10, 12, 13, 15, 15, 16, 17, 18.

It does indeed appear that $M_E > M_C$ in general because six of the seven experimental sample scores are larger than all of the seven control sample scores. A way of determining whether this is a statistically significant outcome is to assign ranks 1 to 14 to the arrayed scores and sum the ranks of the two groups. The rank sums and means are

$$T_E = 5 + 9 + 10.5 + 10.5 + 12 + 13 + 14 = 74, \overline{T}_E = 10.57$$

and

$$T_C = 1 + 2 + 3 + 4 + 6 + 7 + 8 = 31, \overline{T}_C = 4.43.$$

If the null hypothesis H_0: $M_E = M_C$ is true, the two average rank sums should be about equal. The average rank sum for the experimental group is much larger than that for the control group. We will see later how to determine that the P-value for an outcome this extreme is .002. We reject the null hypothesis at the .05 level and conclude that the experimental group has a larger median score than the control group.

The test carried out in this example is called the Mann-Whitney U test or the Wilcoxon rank sum test. The MINITAB and SPSSX solutions to Example 4.1 are shown in Figures 4.1 and 4.2. The MINITAB command is "Mann-Whitney 1," where the 1 requests a one-tailed test in the positive direction. The $W = 74$ corresponds to our $T_E = 74$. The one-tailed P-value of .0036 is based on the normal approximation with a continuity correction, both with and without an adjustment for ties. The normal approximation is not very good for sample sizes as small as we have here. The ETA1 and ETA2 on the printout are the Greek letters η_1 and η_2, which denote the respective population medians.

The SPSSX package solution gives the exact two-tailed P-value of .0041, which corresponds to a one-tailed P-value of .002, as we found. This package also gives a one-tailed $P = .003$ based on the normal approximation. This value does not agree with the MINITAB solution. The difference lies in the fact that SPSSX includes a correction for ties but does not include a continuity correction; MINITAB includes both.

We will now develop the *Mann-Whitney-Wilcoxon test* in general.

Assume that $X_1, X_2, \ldots, X_{n_1}$, and $Y_1, Y_2, \ldots, Y_{n_2}$ are two independent random samples measured on at least an ordinal scale and drawn from any continuous distributions (not necessarily symmetric) with medians M_X and M_Y, respectively. We want to test the null hypothesis that these unknown medians are equal, or

$$H_0: M_X = M_Y.$$

```
MTB >   read E into c1 and C into c2
DATA>   15 10
DATA>   18 5
DATA>   8 4
DATA>   15 9
DATA>   17 12
DATA>   16 6
DATA>   13 7
DATA>   end
        7 ROWS READ
MTB >   name c1='E'
MTB >   name c2='C'
MTB >   mann-whitney   1 c1    c2


Mann-Whitney Confidence Interval and Test

E           N = 7       Median =    15.000
C           N = 7       Median =     7.000
Point estimate for ETA1-ETA2 is   8.000
95.9 pct c.i. for ETA1-ETA2 is (3.002,11.000)
W = 74.0
Test of ETA1 = ETA2 vs. ETA1 g.t. ETA2 is significant at
0.0036
The test is significant at 0.0036 (adjusted for ties)
```

Figure 4.1. MINITAB Solution to Example 4.1

If the distributions of X and Y are assumed to be the same except for possible differences in location, the distributions are identical under the null hypothesis.

The test procedure that is most appropriate for this situation is to pool the $n_1 + n_2 = N$ observations into a single ordered array while keeping track of whether each is an X or Y observation. Thus the array of a sample of $n_1 = 3$ and $n_2 = 4$ might be recorded as $XXXYYYY$. This array shows that the three smallest observations come from the X population and the four largest come from the Y population. This is the most extreme case to support the alternative $A_-: M_X < M_Y$. Thus we see that the relative positions of the X's and Y's in the resulting array of the pooled observations give us information about the relative values of their population medians. One way to compare the relative positions is to assign the ranks $1, 2, \ldots, N$ to the arrayed observations to reflect their relative magnitudes. The *Mann-Whitney-Wilcoxon test* statistic is

```
data list /group 1 score 3-4
npar tests m-w = score by group (0,1)
begin data
0 15
0 18
0 8
0 15
0 17
0 16
0 13
1 10
1 5
1 4
1 9
1 12
1 6
1 7
end data
```

```
- - - - - Mann-Whitney U - Wilcoxon Rank Sum W Test
    SCORE
by GROUP

    Mean Rank       Cases

       10.57           7   GROUP = E
        4.43           7   GROUP = C
                      ─
                      14  Total
                                Exact        Corrected for ties
          U       W      2-Tailed P    Z       2-Tailed P
        3.0     74.0        .0041    -2.7502      .0060
```

Figure 4.2. SPSSX Solution to Example 4.1

$$T_X = \text{sum of the } X \text{ ranks,}$$

that is, the sum of the ranks assigned to the X observations in the pooled array. A large value of T_X supports the alternative A_+: $M_X > M_Y$ and calls for a right-tail P-value. A small value of T_X supports A_-: $M_X < M_Y$ and calls for a left-tail P-value. With the alternative A: $M_X \neq M_Y$ we double the smaller one-tail P-value.

The null distribution of T_X is given in Table D, Appendix A, for $n_1 \leq n_2 \leq 10$. Given that the table covers only $n_1 \leq n_2$, the sample with fewer observations must be labeled X. For a given n_1, n_2, the entry in the column labeled P is the left-tail P-value for the corresponding entry in the column labeled Left T_X and also the right-tail P-value for the entry in the column labeled Right T_X. For example, with $n_1 = 6$, $n_2 = 8$, the entry $P = .054$ represents $\Pr(T_X \leq 32)$ and also $\Pr(T_X \geq 58)$. For larger sample sizes, the normal approximation to the distribution of T_X can be used. The appropriate test statistics are

$$Z_{X,L} = \frac{T_X + .5 - n_1(N+1)/2}{\sqrt{n_1 n_2 (N+1)/12}} \qquad Z_{X,R} = \frac{T_X - .5 - n_1(N+1)/2}{\sqrt{n_1 n_2 (N+1)/12}}, \qquad (4.1)$$

where $Z_{X,L}$ is used to find a left-tail P-value and $Z_{X,R}$ is used to find a right-tail P-value from Table A, Appendix A. With a two-sided alternative, the P-value is twice the right-tail probability for Z where Z is defined as

$$Z = \begin{cases} -Z_{X,L} & \text{if } T_X < n_1(N+1)/2 \\ Z_{X,R} & \text{if } T_X > n_1(N+1)/2 \end{cases}$$

If ties occur between or within samples, each tied observation should be assigned its midrank.

Now we will examine how the entries in Table D can be obtained when the sample sizes are small. Consider the case where $n_1 = 2$, $n_2 = 3$. We know that the ranks must be 1, 2, 3, 4, and 5, and hence the only issue is how these ranks are allocated between the X and Y samples. There are $\binom{5}{2} = 10$ different ways of allocating the five ranks to the two groups and each different way is equally likely under the null hypothesis; therefore, each one has probability 1/10. Table 4.1 shows these allocations and the resultant values calculated for the test statistic T_X. From Table 4.1 we see that $\Pr(T_X \leq 4) = 2/10$ and $\Pr(T_X \leq 5) = 4/10$, which agree with the corresponding entries in Table D.

Example 4.2

Fourqurcan (1987) describes an experiment conducted to show that the K-ABC test, a new test for measuring limited English proficiency, is better than the WISC-R, an older, established test. The primary comparison involved results on the WISC-R Full Scale IQ and the K-ABC Mental Processing Composite tests for Latino learning-disabled children. For a

TABLE 4.1
Possible Allocations of Ranks

X Ranks	Y Ranks	Value of T_X	Probability
1, 2	3, 4, 5	3	1/10
1, 3	2, 4, 5	4	1/10
1, 4	2, 3, 5	5	1/10
2, 3	1, 4, 5	5	1/10
2, 4	1, 3, 5	6	1/10
1, 5	2, 3, 4	6	1/10
2, 5	1, 3, 4	7	1/10
3, 4	1, 2, 5	7	1/10
3, 5	1, 2, 4	8	1/10
4, 5	1, 2, 3	9	1/10

study on a smaller scale, suppose 24 such children are divided randomly into two groups of 12 each. One group is given the WISC-R test and the other is given the K-ABC test; the simulated scores shown below represent the results. The K-ABC test is to be judged better if it produces higher median scores than the WISC-R test on the average.

WISC-R: 96, 67, 87, 59, 77, 88, 76, 75, 74, 66, 79, 80

K-ABC: 91, 71, 89, 83, 78, 95, 73, 97, 98, 97, 99, 99

SOLUTION TO EXAMPLE 4.2:
MANN-WHITNEY-WILCOXON TEST

Since $n_1 = n_2 = 12$, either group can be labeled X. Call X the WISC-R scores; the null hypothesis is H_0: $M_X = M_Y$ and the alternative is A_-: $M_X < M_Y$, which calls for a left-tail P-value. The 24 observations are pooled in a single array, with X underlined, and assigned ranks 1 to 24, as shown in Table 4.2. The sum of the X ranks is $T_X = 107$. The correct test statistic from Equation 4.1 is $Z_{X,L}$, which we calculate as

$$Z_{X,L} = \frac{107 + .5 - 12(25)/2}{\sqrt{12(12)(25)/12}} = -2.45.$$

The left-tail P-value from Table A, Appendix A, is $P = .0071$, and therefore we reject the null hypothesis, as the authors did in the original study using a parametric test.

TABLE 4.2
Scores on Tests

Observed Value	Rank
59	1
66	2
67	3
71	4
73	5
74	6
75	7
76	8
77	9
78	10
79	11
80	12
83	13
87	14
88	15
89	16
91	17
95	18
96	19
97	20.5
97	20.5
98	22
99	23.5
99	23.5

The MINITAB and SPSSX solutions to Example 4.2 appear in Figures 4.3 and 4.4. The -1 in the MINITAB Mann-Whitney command indicates a one-tailed test in the negative direction. The solution with $P = .0071$ based on the normal approximation agrees with ours; it has a continuity correction but no correction for ties. The MINITAB solution with $P = .0070$ has both a continuity correction and a correction for ties. The SPSSX solution gives an exact one-tailed P-value of $.0121/2 = .006$, which comes from a table like Table D, Appendix A, that includes larger n_1 and n_2. The one-tailed $P = .0130/2 = .0065$ based on the normal approximation does not agree with the MINITAB solution because, although it has a correction for ties, it does not have a continuity correction.

The test based on the sum of X ranks was proposed by Wilcoxon and called the *Wilcoxon rank sum test*. An equivalent test statistic was

38

```
MTB >    read X into c1 and Y into c2
DATA>    96 91
DATA>    67 71
DATA>    87 89
DATA>    59 83
DATA>    77 78
DATA>    88 95
DATA>    76 73
DATA>    75 97
DATA>    74 98
DATA>    66 97
DATA>    79 99
DATA>    80 99
DATA>    end
     12 ROWS READ
MTB >    name c1='X'
MTB >    name c2='Y'
MTB >    mann-whitney -1 c1 c2

Mann-Whitney Confidence Interval and Test

X            N= 12      Median =    76.50
Y            N= 12      Median =    93.00
Point estimate for ETA1-ETA2 is  -12.50
95.4 pct c.i. for ETA1-ETA2 is   (-22.00,-3.00)
W = 107.0
Test of ETA1 = ETA2 vs. ETA1 1.t. ETA2 is significant at 0.0071
The test is significant at 0.0070 (adjusted for ties)
```

Figure 4.3. MINITAB Solution to Example 4.2

independently proposed by Mann and Whitney. Hence here the test is called the *Mann-Whitney-Wilcoxon test* (with the proposers listed in alphabetical order).

The Mann-Whitney-Wilcoxon rank sum test is the nonparametric alternative to the Student's *t* test for two mutually independent random samples, which requires the assumption of normal distributions with equal variances and data measured on an interval scale. The nonparametric test requires only the assumption of any continuous distributions, no matter what shape, and data measured on an ordinal scale. The asymptotic relative efficiency of this test relative to the Student's *t* test is .955 for normal distributions, 1.00 for the continuous uniform distribution, and at least .864 for any

```
data list /group 1 score 3-4
npar tests m-w = score by group (0,1)
begin data
0  96
0  67
0  87
0  59
0  77
0  88
0  76
0  75
0  74
0  66
0  79
0  80
1  91
1  71
1  89
1  83
1  78
1  95
1  73
1  97
1  98
1  97
1  99
1  99
end data
```

- - - - - Mann-Whitney U - Wilcoxon Rank Sum W Test
    SCORE
by GROUP

Mean Rank	Cases	
8.92	12	GROUP = X
16.08	12	GROUP = Y
	24	Total

		Exact	Corrected for ties	
U	W	2-Tailed P	Z	2-Tailed P
29.0	107.0	.0121	-2.4837	.0130

Figure 4.4. SPSSX Solution to Example 4.2

continuous distribution, and is larger than 1.00 for some heavy-tailed distributions.

The endpoints of the confidence interval estimate of $M_X - M_Y$ that correspond to the Mann-Whitney-Wilcoxon test for two independent samples are the kth from the smallest and kth from the largest of the $n_1 n_2$ differences $X_i - Y_j$, $i = 1, 2, \ldots, n_1$, $j = 1, 2, \ldots, n_2$. The value of k for large sample sizes is

$$k = .5 + n_1 n_2 / 2 - Z_{\alpha/2} \sqrt{n_1 n_2 (n_1 + n_2 + 1)/12}, \qquad (4.2)$$

rounded down to the next smaller integer. For small sample sizes the value of k is found from Table D, Appendix A, in a manner similar to that used in Chapter 3 for Tables B and C. Here, for confidence coefficient $1 - 2P$, k is the rank of that entry in the column labeled Left T_X in Table D for the given n_1, n_2 that corresponds to an entry of the value P in the column labeled P. For example, with $n_1 = 6$, $n_2 = 8$, confidence level $1 - 2(.021) = .958$, the corresponding Left T_X entry is 29, which has rank 9. Thus $k = 9$, and the confidence interval endpoints are the ninth smallest and largest of the 6(8) = 48 differences $X_i - Y_j$.

Example 4.3

Borod, Caron, and Koff (1984) report on an experiment designed to compare performance and preference measures of lateral dominance for left-handed and right-handed persons. Each subject carried out 10 objective tests of performance, once using the right hand and once using the left hand, and received a score based on performance using each hand. Each score was converted to a dominance ratio by taking the score using the dominant side minus the score for the other side and dividing this difference by the sum of the scores. A preference test determined the dominant side as right for right-handed subjects and left for left-handed subjects. The dominance ratios range between −1 and +1, with zero representing equal strength in performance, a positive value meaning more skill or strength using the dominant side, and a negative value meaning the opposite. The data below are dominance ratios for samples of five left-handed (L) subjects and six right-handed (R) subjects. Find a confidence interval estimate (using about 95% confidence) for the difference in medians $M_L - M_R$.

L: −.002, .005, .020, .025, .040

TABLE 4.3
Calculation of Differences

L	R	.010	.020	.032	.070	.132	.320
−.002		−.012	−.022	−.034	−.072	−.134	−.322
.005		−.005	−.015	−.027	−.065	−.127	−.315
.020		.010	0	−.012	−.050	−.112	−.300
.025		.015	.005	−.007	−.045	−.107	−.295
.040		.030	.020	.008	−.030	−.092	−.280

R: .010, .020, .032, .070, .132, .320

SOLUTION TO EXAMPLE 4.3:
MANN-WHITNEY-WILCOXON TEST

Since the L group has the smaller sample size, we label it as X and the R group as Y; this makes $n_1 = 5$, $n_2 = 6$. Table D, Appendix A, shows that $P = .026$ is possible, and this gives a confidence level of $1 - 2(.026) = .948$, which is close to .95. The corresponding rank of Left T is five, so $k = 5$. We find the 30 differences $X - Y$ (L − R) in Table 4.3 in a systematic way by listing the Y (R) observations across the top row from smallest to largest and the X (L) observations down the first column also from smallest to largest. Each entry in Table 4.3, then, is the corresponding column minus row difference.

Notice that each row and column in Table 4.3 is an ordered array, so that it is relatively easy to identify the fifth-smallest and fifth-largest entries as −.280 and .008, respectively. The confidence interval estimate is $-.280 \le M_L - M_R \le .008$. Note that this interval includes zero, so that we cannot conclude that the median difference of dominance ratios is significantly different from zero.

The first MINITAB solution to Example 4.3 requests 94% confidence, which uses $k = 5$ and the exact same confidence interval endpoints as ours, but they show the confidence coefficient as 94.5 based on the normal approximation instead of the correct value 94.8. The other MINITAB solutions request 95%, 96.4%, and 94.8% confidence, respectively; all solutions use $k = 4$ and give the normal approximation confidence level as 96.4%. Apparently the package adopts the conservative approach of giving an interval with at least the requested confidence coefficient.

```
MTB >    set L into c1
DATA>    -0.002 0.005 0.02 0.025 0.04
MTB >    set R into c2
DATA>    0.01 0.02 0.032 0.07 0.132 0.32
DATA>    end
MTB >    name c1='L'
MTB >    name c2='R'
MTB >    mann-whitney 94 c1 c2
```

Mann-Whitney Confidence Interval and Test

```
L        N = 5      Median =      0.0200
R        N = 6      Median =      0.0510
Point estimate for ETA1-ETA2 is   -0.0320
94.5 pct c.i. for ETA1-ETA2 is (-0.2800,0.0080)
W = 21.5
Test of ETA1 = ETA2 vs. ETA1 n.e. ETA2 is significant at 0.1441
The test is significant at 0.1432 (adjusted for ties)
```

Cannot reject at alpha = 0.05

```
MTB >    mann-whitney 95 c1 c2
```

Mann-Whitney Confidence Interval and Test

```
L        N = 5      Median =      0.0200
R        N = 6      Median =      0.0510
Point estimate for ETA1-ETA2 is   -0.0320
96.4 pct c.i. for ETA1-ETA2 is (-0.2950,0.0100)
W = 21.5
Test of ETA1 = ETA2 vs. ETA1 n.e. ETA2 is significant at 0.1441
The test is significant at 0.1432 (adjusted for ties)
```

Cannot reject at alpha = 0.05

Figure 4.5. MINITAB Solution to Example 4.3 (page 1 of 2)

5. LOCATION TESTS AND MULTIPLE COMPARISONS FOR $k \geq 3$ MUTUALLY INDEPENDENT SAMPLES (KRUSKAL-WALLIS TEST)

This chapter extends the two-sample Mann-Whitney-Wilcoxon test discussed in Chapter 4 to the case of three or more mutually independent samples. With three or more samples, confidence interval estimates of the individual pairs of differences are not used, because the overall

```
MTB >  mann-whitney 96.4 c1 c2

Mann-Whitney Confidence Interval and Test

L          N =  5     Median =     0.0200
R          N =  6     Median =     0.0510
Point estimate for ETA1-ETA2 is  -0.0320
94.4 pct c.i. for ETA1-ETA2 is (-0.2950,0.0100)
W = 21.5
Test of ETA1 = ETA2 vs. ETA1 n.e. ETA2 is significant at 0.1441
The test is significant at 0.1432 (adjusted for ties)

Cannot reject at alpha = 0.05


MTB >  mann-whitney 94.8 c1 c2

Mann-Whitney Confidence Interval and Test

L          N =  5     Median =     0.0200
R          N =  6     Median =     0.0510
Point estimate for ETA1-ETA2 is  -0.0320
96.4 pct c.i. for ETA1-ETA2 is (-0.2950,0.0100)
W = 21.5
Test of ETA1 = ETA2 vs. ETA1 n.e. ETA2 is significant at 0.1441
The test is significant at 0.1432 (adjusted for ties)

Cannot reject at alpha = 0.05
```

Figure 4.5. MINITAB Solution to Example 4.3 (page 2 of 2)

significance level is not controlled. Rather, paired comparisons with a single overall level are used. The nonparametric procedures described here correspond to the classical one-way ANOVA and Bonferroni multiple comparisons procedures, which require the assumption of normal distributions with equal variances.

Example 5.1

Taylor, Ziegler, and Partenio (1984) describe a study undertaken to compare the discrepancy between Verbal IQ scores and Performance IQ scores computed from the WISC-R test (called the VP discrepancy) for three different ethnic groups: white, black, and Hispanic. They found the average discrepancy (regardless of direction) to be considerably larger for Hispanics than for either of the other ethnic groups, and

44

TABLE 5.1
VP Scores

Black	Hispanic	White
1 10	4 17	2 12
3 11	5 22	3 14
6 16	12 27	5 18
7 20	13 29	8 23
9 21	15 30	10 25

average scores for blacks and whites to be about the same. The subjects were a stratified sample of 555 children ages 6-11 years in the state of Florida. Suppose a small-scale replica of this study produced the VP scores shown in Table 5.1, with 10 scores (artificial data) for each group. Are the conclusions the same?

SOLUTION TO EXAMPLE 5.1:
KRUSKAL-WALLIS TEST

If the VP scores for all three groups have the same distribution, the data can be regarded as a single sample of 30 observations and the ethnic groups represented will be randomly distributed in an ordered array of these 30 observations. If, on the other hand, Hispanics, say, have larger VP scores on the average, the Hispanic scores will tend to be the larger ones in this array. We form the array of 30 scores with ethnic group designation in Table 5.2 and assign ranks 1 to 30, using midranks for ties.

Table 5.3 shows how the $N = 30$ ranks are distributed among the ethnic groups and the rank sums for each group. The sum of all N ranks is $N(N + 1)/2 = 465$. If the ranks are randomly distributed among ethnic groups, each rank sum would be about equal to $465/3 = 155$. We measure the discrepancy by taking the sum of squares of deviations between the actual rank sums and this value 155, or

$$(126 - 155)^2 + (196 - 155)^2 + (143 - 155)^2 = 2,666.$$

The test statistic is a function of this sum of squares and is $Q = 3.44$, as will be shown later. This result is referred to a chi-square table, given here as Table E, Appendix A, with 2 degrees of freedom to find $P > .10$. Our results do not show significant differences in VP scores among the

TABLE 5.2
Calculations From Table 5.1

Score	Ethnic Group	Rank
1	B	1
2	W	2
3	B	3.5
3	W	3.5
4	H	5
5	H	6.5
5	W	6.5
6	B	8
7	B	9
8	W	10
9	B	11
10	B	12.5
10	W	12.5
11	B	14
12	H	15.5
12	W	15.5
13	H	17
14	W	18
15	H	19
16	B	20
17	H	21
18	W	22
20	B	23
21	B	24
22	H	25
23	W	26
25	W	27
27	H	28
29	H	29
30	H	30

TABLE 5.3
Calculation of Rank Sums

	Black		Hispanic		White	
	1	12.5	5	21	2	15.5
	3.5	14	6.5	25	3.5	18
	8	20	15.5	28	6.5	22
	9	23	17	29	10	26
	11	24	19	30	12.5	27
Rank sum	126		196		143	

three ethnic groups. This conclusion is not the same as that found in the published study based on parametric procedures, but the data there were different also.

The MINITAB and SPSSX solutions to Example 5.1 are shown in Figures 5.1 and 5.2. All answers agree. Notice that the change in the value of the test statistic after adjustment for ties is negligible, as is generally the case.

This example illustrates the nonparametric *Kruskal-Wallis test,* or nonparametric one-way ANOVA test. In general, assume we have k mutually independent random samples measured on at least an ordinal scale and drawn from any continuous distributions (not necessarily symmetric) that are identical except for central location, as measured by, say, the medians $M_1, M_2, \ldots M_k$. The null hypothesis is that these medians are equal, or

$$H_0: M_1 = M_2 = \ldots = M_k.$$

The alternative here is always that the medians are not all the same, and this is a two-sided alternative A. When the k distributions are assumed the same except for possible differences in location, all distributions are identical under H_0.

The test procedure is to pool all N observations into a single ordered array and rank them from 1 to N while keeping track of which sample produced which observation. The sample sizes need not be equal here, and we denote the sample sizes by $n_1, n_2, \ldots, n_k$, with the total number of observations being $N = n_1 + n_2 + \ldots + n_k$. Then the ranks assigned to each sample are summed to get the individual rank sums $R_1, R_2, \ldots, R_k$.

Note that R_i is the sum of the n_i ranks assigned to sample i and that $R_1 + R_2 + \ldots + R_k = 1 + 2 + \ldots + N = N(N+1)/2$. Under H_0, the ranks entering the sum R_i are a random sample of n_i of the possible ranks, and we expect the average rank sums $\overline{R}_i = R_i/n_i$ to be about equal to each other and to the expected rank of any observation that is $[N(N+1)/2]/N = (N+1)/2$. The test statistic then is a function of the weighted sum of squares of deviations of the actual average rank sums from the expected average rank sum.

The *Kruskal-Wallis test statistic* is

$$Q = \frac{12 \sum_{i=1}^{k} n_i \left(\overline{R}_i - \frac{N+1}{2} \right)^2}{N(N+1)} = \frac{12}{N(N+1)} \sum_{i=1}^{k} \frac{R_i^2}{n_i} - 3(N+1). \qquad (5.1)$$

```
MTB >   read VP score into c1, code ETHNIC for score into c2
DATA>   1   1
DATA>   3   1
DATA>   6   1
DATA>   7   1
DATA>   9   1
DATA>   10  1
DATA>   11  1
DATA>   16  1
DATA>   20  1
DATA>   21  1
DATA>   4   2
DATA>   5   2
DATA>   12  2
DATA>   13  2
DATA>   15  2
DATA>   17  2
DATA>   22  2
DATA>   27  2
DATA>   29  2
DATA>   30  2
DATA>   2   3
DATA>   3   3
DATA>   5   3
DATA>   8   3
DATA>   10  3
DATA>   12  3
DATA>   14  3
DATA>   18  3
DATA>   23  3
DATA>   25  3
DATA>   end
        30 ROWS READ
MTB kruskal wallis for data in c1 subscripts    in c2

LEVEL   NOBS    MEDIAS AVE. RANK   Z VALUE
    1     10     9.500      12.6    -1.28
    2     10    16.000      19.6     1.80
    3     10    11.000      14.3    -0.53
OVERALL 30                 15.5

H = 3.44   d.f. = 2   p = 0.180
H = 3.44   d.f. = 2   p = 0.179 (adj. for ties)
```

Figure 5.1. MINITAB Solution to Example 5.1

The latter form of the test statistic in Equation 5.1 is easiest for purposes of calculation. A table of the exact null distribution of Q is given here

```
data list /vp score 1-2 group 4
npar tests k-w = score by group (1,3)
begin data
1   1
3   1
6   1
7   1
9   1
10  1
11  1
16  1
20  1
21  1
4   2
5   2
12  2
13  2
15  2
17  2
22  2
27  2
29  2
30  2
2   3
3   3
5   3
8   3
10  3
12  3
14  3
18  3
23  3
25  3
end data
```

- - - - - Kruskal-Wallis 1-Way Anova
      SCORE
by GROUP

Mean Rank	Cases	
12.60	10	GROUP = Black
19.60	10	GROUP = Hispanic
14.30	10	GROUP = White
	30	Total

Cases	Chi-Square	Significance	Corrected for ties Chi-Square	Significance
30	3.4400	.1791	3.4431	.1788

Figure 5.2. SPSSX Solution to Example 5.1

as Table F, Appendix A, for $k = 3$, each $n_i \leq 5$. For large sample sizes, Q is approximately chi-square distributed with $k - 1$ degrees of freedom, given here as Table E, Appendix A. Since small values of Q support H_0, the approximate P-value is right tail from Table E or F.

The Kruskal-Wallis test can be used if $k = 2$ and the alternative is two-sided; it is then equivalent to the Mann-Whitney-Wilcoxon test statistic based on the normal approximation. If $k = 2$ and the alternative is one-sided, the Mann-Whitney-Wilcoxon test must be used instead.

When the null hypothesis of equal medians is rejected, we may not be content with the conclusion that the medians are different. We may want to make more specific inferences about how the medians differ. With a total of k medians, there are $k(k - 1)/2$ possible pairwise comparisons that can be made among the populations. A statistical technique for making all $k(k - 1)/2$ pairwise comparisons and controlling the overall error rate is called multiple comparisons. The overall error rate is the probability that at least one of the inferences is incorrect if the null hypothesis is true. (The comparisons need not be pairwise, but only this case is illustrated.)

We do not have an exact nonparametric statistical technique for pairwise comparisons, but we do have an approximate procedure (based on Bonferroni inequalities) that can be used with large sample sizes. The method is to declare that M_i is significantly different from M_j if the average rank sums for those respective groups satisfy the inequality

$$|\bar{R}_i - \bar{R}_j| > Z_c \sqrt{\frac{N(N+1)}{12}\left(\frac{1}{n_i} + \frac{1}{n_j}\right)}, \qquad (5.2)$$

where Z_c comes from the standard normal distribution but not in the usual way. With a total of c pairwise comparisons and an overall level of α, Z_c is the critical value that corresponds to a right-tail P-value of $\alpha/2c$. The values of Z_c to use in Equation 5.2 are given here in Table H, Appendix A, as a function of c and α. The value of c is usually equal to $k(k - 1)/2$, but it can be a smaller value. This multiple comparisons procedure is illustrated with Example 5.2.

Example 5.2

McCabe (1987) reports on a study designed to examine performance by adults on relatively simple tasks of class-inclusion reasoning under

50

TABLE 5.4
Numbers of Correct Answers

Group I	Group II	Group III
5	5	8
6	6	9
7	7	7
3	4	8
4	5	
5	6	

time pressure conditions. The subjects were randomly selected university students in psychology. The research hypothesis was that adults who respond more quickly to class-inclusion questions will give more incorrect answers than will slower responders. Two types of arrays were presented on slides. One type consisted of two shapes of a single color, such as two green circles and five green squares. The appropriate class-inclusion question for this type of array would be, "Are there more squares than green?" The second type consisted of a single shape but two colors, such as two orange and seven purple squares, accompanied by the class-inclusion question, "Are there more purple than squares?"

The subjects were divided randomly into three groups to view the slides and respond to the corresponding class-inclusion questions. Group I subjects were given a limited viewing time and told to respond as quickly as possible. Groups II and III subjects were given no instructions regarding speed, but Group II had limited viewing time for each slide; slide exposure for Group III was terminated only after the subject responded to the corresponding class-inclusion question. Table 5.4 shows simulated data representing the number of correct answers for 10 slides shown to each of 16 subjects divided randomly into the three groups. Determine whether the median numbers of correct answers are the same for the three groups and, if not, carry out all possible pairwise comparisons.

SOLUTION TO EXAMPLE 5.2:
KRUSKAL-WALLIS TEST

We rank the data in Table 5.4 from 1 to 16, with midranks for ties, as shown in Table 5.5, sum the ranks for each group, and compute the average rank sums.

TABLE 5.5
Calculation of Rank Sums

	Group I	Group II	Group III
	5.5	5.5	14.5
	9.0	9.0	16.0
	12.0	12.0	12.0
	1.0	2.5	14.5
	2.5	5.5	
	5.5	9.0	
Sum	35.5	43.5	57.9
Average	5.92	7.25	14.25

The sum of ranks for all three groups combined is $N(N + 1)/2 = 136$. If the null hypothesis is true, the average rank sums for the three groups will be equal to the grand mean of all groups combined, or $136/16 = 8.5$. The test statistic is a function of the weighted sum of squares of deviations of the average rank sums about this value 8.5; the weights are the corresponding sample sizes. This weighted sum of squares is

$$6(5.92 - 8.5)^2 + 6(7.25 - 8.5)^2 + 4(14.25 - 8.5)^2 = 181.5634.$$

The Kruskal-Wallis test statistic in Equation 5.1 is found by multiplying this weighted sum of squares by the constant $12/16(17) = .04412$ to get $Q = 8.01$. The significance of $Q = 8.01$ is determined by comparing it to a chi-square value with 2 degrees of freedom. The corresponding P-value from Table E, Appendix A, is $.01 < P < .02$, so we reject the null hypothesis and conclude that the medians differ for the three groups. McCabe also used the Kruskal-Wallis test, but she found $P > .10$ for different data and concluded that the medians were the same.

Figures 5.3 and 5.4 show the MINITAB and SPSSX solutions for the Kruskal-Wallis test in Example 5.2. The 8.01 value of the test statistic without the adjustment for ties agrees exactly. The ties in this example are extensive, and the test statistic adjusted for ties reflects this. Both solutions use the chi-square approximation to find the P-value, which is appropriate.

Now we use multiple comparisons to see which medians differ significantly for our simulated data at the overall level .05. The value of Z_c with $c = 3(2)/2 = 3$ and $\alpha = .05$ is 2.394 from Table H, Appendix A.

```
MTB >  read answer into c1, code group for answer into c2
DATA>  5 1
DATA>  6 1
DATA>  7 1
DATA>  3 1
DATA>  4 1
DATA>  5 1
DATA>  5 2
DATA>  6 2
DATA>  7 2
DATA>  4 2
DATA>  5 2
DATA>  6 2
DATA>  8 3
DATA>  9 3
DATA>  7 3
DATA>  8 3
DATA>  end
      16 ROWS READ
MTB >  name c1='answer'
MTB >  kruskal wallis for data in c1 subscripts in c2
```

LEVEL	NOBS	MEDIAN	AVE. RANK	Z VALUE
1	6	5.000	5.9	-1.68
2	6	5.500	7.2	-0.81
3	4	8.000	14.2	2.79
OVERALL	16		8.5	

```
H = 8.01   d.f. = 2   p = 0.018
H = 8.26   d.f. = 2   p = 0.016 (adj. for ties)
```

Figure 5.3. MINITAB Solutoin to Example 5.2

The right-hand side of Equation 5.2 for Groups I and II with $n_1 = n_2 = 6$ is

$$2.394 \sqrt{\frac{16(17)}{12}\left(\frac{1}{6}+\frac{1}{6}\right)} = 6.58.$$

The observed difference of average rank sums for Groups I and II is only $7.25 - 5.92 = 1.33$, so these groups do not differ significantly. The right-hand side of Equation 5.2 for Groups I and III, or Groups II and III, is

```
data list /answer 1 group 4
npar tests k-w = answer by group (1,3)
begin data
5    1
6    1
7    1
3    1
4    1
5    1
5    2
6    2
7    2
4    2

5    2
6    2
8    3
9    3
7    3
8    3
end data
```

```
- - - - - Kruskal-Wallis 1-Way Anova
   ANSWER
by GROUP

     Mean Rank        Cases

         5.92            6    GROUP = 1
         7.25            6    GROUP = 2
        14.25            4    GROUP = 3
0                        ──
0                       16    Total
0                                                Corrected for ties
        Cases   Chi-Square  Significance    Chi-Square  Significance
         16        8.0147        .0182          8.2576        .0161
```

Figure 5.4. SPSSX Solution to Example 5.2

$$2.394 \sqrt{\frac{16(17)}{12}\left(\frac{1}{6}+\frac{1}{4}\right)} = 7.36.$$

The observed the difference of the average rank sums for Groups II and III is $14.25 - 7.25 = 7.00$, so they do not differ significantly. But for

Groups I and III, the observed difference is $14.25 - 5.92 = 8.33$, and therefore we conclude that the medians of these groups differ significantly at the .05 level. This conclusion should not be relied upon, however, because the sample sizes here are really not large enough to use this approximate multiple comparisons procedure.

The Kruskal-Wallis test is the nonparametric alternative to the one-way analysis of variance F test, which requires the assumption of normal distributions with equal variances and requires data measured on at least an interval scale. The Kruskal-Wallis test requires data measured on only an ordinal scale and assumes only continuous distributions. The asymptotic relative efficiency of the Kruskal-Wallis test relative to the F test is .955 for normal distributions, 1.00 for the continuous uniform distribution, at least .864 for any continuous distribution, and it can be larger than 1.00.

6. LOCATION TESTS AND MULTIPLE COMPARISONS FOR $k \geq 3$ RELATED SAMPLES (FRIEDMAN'S TEST)

In the Kruskal-Wallis test discussed in Chapter 5, each subject in the total group of N subjects was assigned randomly to a treatment group, and the null hypothesis of no treatment effects was tested. In this situation we assumed there was no reason to think that any differences observed among the treatment effects would be caused by anything other than the treatments themselves. Now, suppose that there is a factor or condition that we fear may confound the effect of the treatments. For example, suppose a psychologist wants to compare four different techniques for measuring responses of 20 students to a specified psychological stimulus. If the techniques have different scales of measurement—for example, technique A is measured on a scale from 0 to 100, while technique B is measured on a scale from 1 to 5—comparisons of the relative magnitude of response to A with response to B makes no sense. Rather, we should divide the 20 students into five groups of 4 each, apply technique A randomly to 1 student in each of the five groups, and compare the responses to technique A with each other.

Alternatively, suppose the measurement scales are the same but the 20 students differ in many ways (intelligence, socioeconomic background, sex, and so on) and hence cannot be expected to respond alike even if treated alike. Then the responses will be more directly comparable if the students are matched as closely as possible into five groups of 4 students each. Since the students within each group are as alike as possible, the techniques can be compared within each group but should not be compared between groups. An alternative situation occurs if the measurement scales are the same and the 20 students are very similar, but the four techniques can be administered only to one set of subjects at a time under the same conditions.

In general, we are talking about a situation in which we want to compare T treatments using a design where the $N = BT$ subjects are matched into B groups, each of size $N/B = T$, the T subjects within each group are assigned randomly to the T treatments, the treatment effects are measured on at least an ordinal scale, and the comparisons of treatment effects are made only within each group. This corresponds to the T treatment *repeated measures design* of classical ANOVA procedures, where the order in which the treatments are assigned is done randomly for each subject (also called the *two-way ANOVA with one observation per cell* and the *randomized complete block design*). Comparisons of the treatment effects are made by ranking the responses to the treatments by the subjects within each group from one to T. No comparisons are made between groups.

The null hypothesis is that the median treatment effects $M_1, M_2, \ldots, M_T$ of the T continuous populations are all the same, that is,

$$H_0: M_1 = M_2 = \ldots = M_T,$$

against the alternative that they are not all the same. Under this null hypothesis the rankings in each group are a random permutation of the integers $1, 2, \ldots, T$ and the sums of the ranks assigned to each treatment will tend to be equal to each other. Since the total sum of ranks is $BT(T + 1)/2$, this common value for each of the T treatments is equal to $B(T + 1)/2$. Thus the test statistic is a function of the sum of squares of the deviations between the treatment rank sums $R_1, R_2, \ldots, R_T$ and $B(T + 1)/2$, or

$$S = \sum_{t=1}^{T} \left[R_t - \frac{B(T+1)}{2} \right]^2 = \sum_{t=1}^{T} R_t^2 - B^2 T(T+1)^2/4. \qquad (6.1)$$

The null distribution of S is given here as Table G, Appendix A, for $B \leq 8$ with $T = 3$ and $B \leq 4$ with $T = 4$. A large value of S calls for rejection of H_0, so the appropriate P-value is the right tail. For larger sample sizes, we calculate S as in Equation 6.1 and substitute the result into

$$Q = 12S/BT(T + 1). \tag{6.2}$$

The distribution of Q is approximately chi-square with $T - 1$ degrees of freedom, so the approximate P-value is a right-tail probability from Table E, Appendix A. The test based on S or Q is called the *Friedman test*.

If the null hypothesis of equal medians is rejected, we may want to estimate the order of effectiveness of the treatments. This estimated order corresponds to the order of magnitude of the treatment rank sums $R_1, R_2, \ldots, R_T$ and is the least squares estimate.

If the sample sizes are large (say, at least 15 each) and the null hypothesis of equal medians is rejected, we can also determine which medians differ significantly by carrying out a multiple comparisons procedure at an overall level α. The medians of treatment groups j and j' are declared to be significantly different if their respective treatment rank sums satisfy the inequality

$$\mid R_j - R_{j'} \mid > Z_c \sqrt{BT(T + 1)/6}\,, \tag{6.3}$$

where Z_c comes from Table H, Appendix A, with T, B, and $c = T(T - 1)/2$ if all possible pairwise comparisons are made. Other post hoc contrasts can also be made.

Example 6.1

Hartley (1973) examined the effects of noise on the performance of tasks by humans. Each subject faced five neon bulbs arranged in the form of a pentagon and five correspondingly arranged metal contacts. The subject was asked to touch the contact that corresponded to a particular bulb. This action would light another bulb, and the subject was then supposed to touch the contact corresponding to the newly lit bulb, and so on. In one part of the experiment the subjects were required to do the task for two 20-minute intervals. The design was a randomized complete block and the data given in the article were the mean numbers of errors made in each 5-minute block of time for the latter 20-minute test. During each 20-minute interval the surroundings were either quiet or noisy in each possible combination. For example, Q-N indicates the first 20-minute test was administered under

TABLE 6.1
Mean Test Scores

| Group | Quiet-Noise Combination | | | |
	Q-Q	Q-N	N-Q	N-N
1	5.54	5.31	7.85	6.92
2	5.62	6.15	9.15	10.54
3	5.54	6.31	9.07	10.69
4	6.46	7.23	8.00	8.62

quiet conditions and the second test under noisy conditions. Use the data in Table 6.1 to test the null hypothesis that the four quiet-noise combinations of surroundings produce the same median number of errors.

SOLUTION TO EXAMPLE 6.1: FRIEDMAN'S TEST

The four quiet-noise combination are the treatments here, so we have $T = 4$ treatments and $B = 4$ groups. We rank the measures of error (the treatment effects) from 1 to 4 in each group and sum the ranks for each treatment, as shown in Table 6.2.

The test statistic from Equation 6.1 is $S = 68$. Table G, Appendix A, shows that the P-value is .0027; therefore, we reject H_0 and conclude that the different combinations of quiet and noise do tend to produce different median error rates in task performance. The estimated ranking of treatment effects from smallest to largest number of errors is Q-Q, Q-N, N-Q, N-N. Since the sample sizes here are only four, we do not have enough observations to justify using the multiple comparisons procedure described in Equation 6.3. However, the procedure is presented here for illustrative purposes.

TABLE 6.2
Calculation of Rank Sums

Block	Q-Q	Q-N	N-Q	N-N
1	2	1	4	3
2	1	2	3	4
3	1	2	3	4
4	1	2	3	4
Sum	5	7	13	15

```
MTB >   read combination in c1 group in c2 and errors in c3
DATA>   1 1 5.54
DATA>   1 2 5.62
DATA>   1 3 5.54
DATA>   1 4 6.46
DATA>   2 1 5.31
DATA>   2 2 6.15
DATA>   2 3 6.31
DATA>   2 4 7.23
DATA>   3 1 7.85
DATA>   3 2 9.15
DATA>   3 3 9.07
DATA>   3 4 8.00
DATA>   4 1 6.92
DATA>   4 2 10.54
DATA>   4 3 10.69
DATA>   4 4 8.62
DATA>   end
     16 ROWS READ
MTB >   name c1='comb'
MTB >   friedman c3 c1 c2

Friedman test of C3 by comb blocked by C2

S = 10.20   d.f. = 3    p = 0.017

                Est.    Sum of
   comb   N   Median    RANKS
      1   4    5.848      5.0
      2   4    6.377      7.0
      3   4    8.767     13.0
      4   4    9.511     15.0

Grand median = 7.626
```

Figure 6.1. MINITAB Solution to Example 6.1

For an overall level of .10, and $c = 6$, Table H, Appendix A, shows that $Z_c = 2.394$. The right-hand side of Equation 6.3 is then equal to $2.394\sqrt{4(4)(5)/6} = 8.74$. The difference between rank sums for the Q-Q and N-N groups is equal to 10, and this is the only difference between groups that exceeds 8.74.

The MINITAB and SPSSX solutions to Example 6.1 are shown in Figures 6.1 and 6.2. Both use the approximate test statistic given in

```
data list /a 1-5 b 7-11 c 13-17 d 19-23
var labels a 'q-q'
           b 'q-n'
           c 'n-q'
           d 'n-n'
npar tests friedman = a b c d
begin data
5.54    5.31    7.85    6.92
5.62    6.15    9.15    10.54
5.54    6.31    9.07    10.69
6.46    7.23    8.00    8.62
end data


- - - - - Friedman Two-Way Anova

    Mean Rank  Variable

         1.25  A        q-q
         1.75  B        q-n
         3.25  C        n-q
         3.75  D        n-n
         Cases          Chi-Square   D.F.   Significance
             4            10.2000      3          .0169
```

Figure 6.2. SPSSX Solution to Example 6.1

Equation 6.2, and the *P*-value of .0169 is based on the chi-square approximation; our *P*-value result of .0027 is exact and is considerably smaller than the approximate *P*-value, which should not be used here. For the MINITAB solution, the data are entered in column c3. Column c2 gives the group number and column c1 gives the quiet-noise combination with 1 = Q-Q, 2 = Q-N, 3 = N-Q, and 4 = N-N.

Example 6.2

Shearer (1982) reports a set of ratings made by newsmen representing CBS, NBC, and ABC about the press-conference behavior of recent U.S. presidents. The performances of the past seven presidents during press conferences were rated on a scale of 1 to 10 (10 = best) on four different attributes, as shown in Table 6.3. Note that these data are measured on an ordinal scale only and hence are not appropriate for a classical analysis of variance test.

60

TABLE 6.3
Ratings of Presidents

	Candor	Informative Value	Combative Skill	Humor
Reagan	6	4	8	8.5
Carter	8	7	6	7
Ford	7	5	4	6
Nixon	5	6	8	4
Johnson	2	3	6	4
Kennedy	5	6	9	9
Eisenhower	8	7	4	3

SOLUTION TO EXAMPLE 6.2: FRIEDMAN'S TEST

If we want to compare the median overall ratings of the seven presidents, we should rank these ratings from 1 to 7 for each attribute separately (1 = worst) and find the totals as shown in Table 6.4. (Note that we do not always rank across rows; it depends on the situation.) This means that the treatments are the presidents and the groups are the attributes, so that $T = 7$ and $B = 4$, and the treatment effects are the overall ratings.

We obtain $S = 129$ from Equation 6.1 and $Q = 6.9107$ from Equation 6.2 with 6 degrees of freedom. From Table E, Appendix A, the right-tail P-value is $.3 < P < .5$, so we conclude there is no difference between median scores for the presidents.

The MINITAB and SPSSX solutions to Example 6.2 are presented in Figures 6.3 and 6.4. Both obtain the value 6.9107, which agrees with ours, and both use the chi-square approximation to find the P-value,

TABLE 6.4
Calculation of Rank Sums

	Candor	Informative Value	Combative Skill	Humor	Total
Reagan	4	2	5.5	6	17.5
Carter	6.5	6.5	3.5	5	21.5
Ford	5	3	1.5	4	13.5
Nixon	2.5	4.5	5.5	2.5	15.0
Johnson	1	1	3.5	2.5	8.0
Kennedy	2.5	4.5	7	7	21.0
Eisenhower	6.5	6.5	1.5	1	15.5

```
MTB >  read president in c1 attribute in c2 and ratings in c3
DATA>  1 1 6
DATA>  1 2 4
DATA>  1 3 8
DATA>  1 4 8.5
DATA>  2 1 8
DATA>  2 2 7
DATA>  2 3 6
DATA>  2 4 7
DATA>  3 1 7
DATA>  3 2 5
DATA>  3 3 4
DATA>  3 4 6
DATA>  4 1 5
DATA>  4 2 6
DATA>  4 3 8
DATA>  4 4 4
DATA>  5 1 2
DATA>  5 2 3
DATA>  5 3 6
DATA>  5 4 4
DATA>  6 1 5
DATA>  6 2 6
DATA>  6 3 9
DATA>  6 4 9
DATA>  7 1 8
DATA>  7 2 7
DATA>  7 3 4
DATA>  7 4 3
DATA>  end
       28 ROWS READ
MTB >  name c1='pres'
MTB >  friedman c3 c1 c2
```

Friedman test of C3 by pres blocked by C2

$S = 6.91$ d.f. $= 6$ $p = 0.330$
$S = 7.17$ d.f. $= 6$ $p = 0.307$ (adjusted for ties)

	pres	N	Est. Median	Sum of RANKS
1	Reagan	4	6.411	17.5
2	Carter	4	6.911	21.5
3	Ford	4	5.482	13.5
4	Nixon	4	5.661	15.0
5	Johnson	4	3.589	8.0
6	Kennedy	4	7.054	21.0
7	Eisenhower	4	5.518	15.5

Grand median $=$ 5.804

Figure 6.3. MINITAB Solution to Example 6.2

```
data list /a 1-3 b 5 c 7 d 9 e 11 f 13 g 15
var labels a 'reagan'
           b 'carter'
           c 'ford'
           d 'nixon'
           e 'johnson'
           f 'kennedy
           g 'eisenhower'
npar tests friedman = a b c d e f g
begin data
6    8 7 5 2 5 8
4    7 5 6 3 6 7
8    6 4 8 6 9 4
8.5 7 6 4 4 9 3
end data
```

- - - - - Friedman Two-Way Anova

Mean Rank	Variable	
4.38	A	reagan
5.38	B	carter
3.38	C	ford
3.75	D	nixon
2.00	E	johnson
5.25	F	kennedy
3.88	G	eisenhower

Cases	Chi-Square	D.F.	Significance
4	6.9107	6	.3292

Figure 6.4. SPSSX Solution to Example 6.2

which is appropriate. The MINITAB solution also gives the test statistic and P-value with the correction for ties.

The Friedman test is the nonparametric alternative to the analysis of variance F test for a single-factor model with a repeated measure. The classical test requires data measured on at least an interval scale and also requires the assumption of normal distributions with equal variances. By contrast, the Friedman test requires data measured on at least an ordinal scale and drawn from any continuous populations, not necessarily normal distributions. The asymptotic relative efficiency of the Friedman test depends on the number of treatments T. Its efficiency relative to the F test is $.955T/(T+1)$ for normal distributions and $T/(T$

+ 1) for the continuous uniform distribution and is always at least .864$T/(T$ + 1) for any continuous distribution. The efficiency is greater than one for some other continuous distributions. For example, it is 3$T/2(T$ + 1) for the double exponential distribution.

7. SUMMARY

When faced with a problem of data analysis, the first step is to decide whether to use a parametric or a nonparametric procedure. A parametric procedure should be used when *both* of the following are true:

1. The data are collected and analyzed using an interval or ratio scale of measurement.
2. All of the assumptions required for the validity of that parametric procedure can be verified.

Otherwise, a nonparametric procedure should be used. This means that a nonparametric procedure is appropriate when any of the following is true:

1. The data are counts or frequencies of different types of outcomes.
2. The data are measured on a nominal scale.
3. The data are measured on an ordinal scale.
4. The assumptions required for the validity of the corresponding parametric procedure are not met or cannot be verified.
5. The shape of the distribution from which the sample is drawn is unknown.
6. The sample size is small.
7. The measurements are imprecise.
8. There are outliers and/or extreme values in the data, making the median more representative than the mean.

This volume has covered five different nonparametric procedures that are appropriate for inferences about location parameters in one or more populations. The sign test and Wilcoxon signed rank test and confidence intervals covered in Chapters 2 and 3 can be used with data on one sample or paired samples. Their corresponding parametric procedure is Student's *t* test and confidence interval. For data on two independent samples, the nonparametric procedure is the Mann-Whitney-Wilcoxon test and confidence interval covered in Chapter 4. The parametric counterpart is the two-sample Student's *t* test. For data on three or more mutually independent samples, the Kruskal-Wallis test discussed in Chapter 5 can be used. The corresponding parametric test is the one-way ANOVA. With three or more related or matched samples, the Friedman test presented in Chapter 6 is appropriate; its parametric counterpart is the two-way ANOVA or one-factor ANOVA with repeated measures.

APPENDIX A: TABLES

TABLE A
Normal Distribution

Table entries are the tail probability, right tail from the value of Z to plus infinity, and also left tail from minus infinity to the value of $-Z$ for all $P \leq .50$, where Z is the standardized normal variable, $Z = (X - \mu)/\sigma$. Read down the first column to the correct first decimal value of Z, and over to the correct column for the second decimal value. The number at the intersection is the value of P.

Z	.00	.01	.02	.03	.04	.05	.06	.07	.08	.09
0.0	.5000	.4960	.4920	.4880	.4840	.4801	.4761	.4721	.4681	.4641
0.1	.4602	.4562	.4522	.4483	.4443	.4404	.4364	.4325	.4286	.4247
0.2	.4207	.4168	.4129	.4090	.4052	.4013	.3974	.3936	.3897	.3859
0.3	.3821	.3783	.3745	.3707	.3669	.3632	.3594	.3557	.3520	.3483
0.4	.3446	.3409	.3372	.3336	.3300	.3264	.3228	.3192	.3156	.3121
0.5	.3085	.3050	.3015	.2981	.2946	.2912	.2877	.2843	.2810	.2776
0.6	.2743	.2709	.2676	.2643	.2611	.2578	.2546	.2514	.2483	.2451
0.7	.2420	.2389	.2358	.2327	.2296	.2266	.2236	.2206	.2177	.2148
0.8	.2119	.2090	.2061	.2033	.2005	.1977	.1949	.1922	.1894	.1867
0.9	.1841	.1814	.1788	.1762	.1736	.1711	.1685	.1660	.1635	.1611
1.0	.1587	.1562	.1539	.1515	.1492	.1469	.1446	.1423	.1401	.1379
1.1	.1357	.1335	.1314	.1292	.1271	.1251	.1230	.1210	.1190	.1170
1.2	.1151	.1131	.1112	.1093	.1075	.1056	.1038	.1020	.1003	.0985
1.3	.0968	.0951	.0934	.0918	.0901	.0885	.0869	.0853	.0838	.0823
1.4	.0808	.0793	.0778	.0764	.0749	.0735	.0721	.0708	.0694	.0681
1.5	.0668	.0655	.0643	.0630	.0618	.0606	.0594	.0582	.0571	.0559
1.6	.0548	.0537	.0526	.0516	.0505	.0495	.0485	.0475	.0465	.0455

continued

TABLE A
Continued

Table entries are the tail probability, right tail from the value of Z to plus infinity, and also left tail from minus infinity to the value of $-Z$ for all $P \le .50$, where Z is the standardized normal variable, $Z = (X - \mu)/\sigma$. Read down the first column to the correct first decimal value of Z, and over to the correct column for the second decimal value. The number at the intersection is the value of P.

Z	.00	.01	.02	.03	.04	.05	.06	.07	.08	.09
1.7	.0446	.0436	.0427	.0418	.0409	.0401	.0392	.0384	.0375	.0367
1.8	.0359	.0351	.0344	.0336	.0329	.0322	.0314	.0307	.0301	.0294
1.9	.0287	.0281	.0274	.0268	.0262	.0256	.0250	.0244	.0239	.0233
2.0	.0228	.0222	.0217	.0212	.0207	.0202	.0197	.0192	.0188	.0183
2.1	.0179	.0174	.0170	.0166	.0162	.0158	.0154	.0150	.0146	.0143
2.2	.0139	.0136	.0132	.0129	.0125	.0122	.0119	.0116	.0113	.0110
2.3	.0107	.0104	.0102	.0099	.0096	.0094	.0091	.0089	.0087	.0084
2.4	.0082	.0080	.0078	.0075	.0073	.0071	.0069	.0068	.0066	.0064
2.5	.0062	.0060	.0059	.0057	.0055	.0054	.0052	.0051	.0049	.0048
2.6	.0047	.0045	.0044	.0043	.0041	.0040	.0039	.0038	.0037	.0036
2.7	.0035	.0034	.0033	.0032	.0031	.0030	.0029	.0028	.0027	.0026
2.8	.0026	.0025	.0024	.0023	.0023	.0022	.0021	.0021	.0020	.0019
2.9	.0019	.0018	.0018	.0017	.0016	.0016	.0015	.0015	.0014	.0014
3.0	.0013	.0013	.0013	.0012	.0012	.0011	.0011	.0011	.0010	.0010
3.1	.0010	.0009	.0009	.0009	.0008	.0008	.0008	.0008	.0007	.0007
3.2	.0007	.0007	.0006	.0006	.0006	.0006	.0006	.0005	.0005	.0005
3.3	.0005	.0005	.0005	.0004	.0004	.0004	.0004	.0004	.0004	.0003
3.4	.0003	.0003	.0003	.0003	.0003	.0003	.0003	.0003	.0003	.0002
3.5	.0002	.0002	.0002	.0002	.0002	.0002	.0002	.0002	.0002	.0002

SOURCE: Adapted from Table V of R. A. Fisher and F. Yates (1963), *Statistical Tables for Biological, Agricultural and Medical Research*, Hafner Publishing Company, New York, with permission of Longman Group Ltd., United Kingdom.

TABLE B
Binomial Distribution With $p = .5$

Entries labeled P in the table are the cumulative probability from each extreme to the value of S, for the given n when $p = .5$. Left-tail probabilities are given for $S \leq .5n$, and right-tail for $S \geq .5n$.

n	Left S	P	Right S	n	Left S	P	Right S	n	Left S	P	Right S
1	0	.5000	1	11	0	.0005	11	16	0	.0000	16
2	0	.2500	2		1	.0059	10		1	.0003	15
	1	.7500	1		2	.0327	9		2	.0021	14
3	0	.1250	3		3	.1133	8		3	.0106	13
	1	.5000	2		4	.2744	7		4	.0384	12
4	0	.0625	4		5	.5000	6		5	.1051	11
	1	.3125	3	12	0	.0002	12		6	.2272	10
	2	.6875	2		1	.0032	11		7	.4018	9
5	0	.0312	5		2	.0193	10		8	.5982	8
	1	.1875	4		3	.0730	9	17	0	.0000	17
	2	.5000	3		4	.1938	8		1	.0001	16
6	0	.0156	6		5	.3872	7		2	.0012	15
	1	.1094	5		6	.6128	6		3	.0064	14
	2	.3438	4	13	0	.0001	13		4	.0245	13
	3	.6562	3		1	.0017	12		5	.0717	12
7	0	.0078	7		2	.0112	11		6	.1662	11
	1	.0625	6		3	.0461	10		7	.3145	10
	2	.2266	5		4	.1334	9		8	.5000	9
	3	.5000	4		5	.2905	8	18	0	.0000	18
8	0	.0039	8		6	.5000	7		1	.0001	17
	1	.0352	7	14	0	.0000	14		2	.0007	16
	2	.1445	6		1	.0009	13		3	.0038	15
	3	.3633	5		2	.0065	12		4	.0154	14
	4	.6367	4		3	.0287	11		5	.0481	13
9	0	.0020	9		4	.0898	10		6	.1189	12
	1	.0195	8		5	.2120	9		7	.2403	11
	2	.0898	7		6	.3953	8		8	.4073	10
	3	.2539	6		7	.6047	7		9	.5927	9
	4	.5000	5	15	0	.0000	15	19	0	.0000	19
10	0	.0010	10		1	.0005	14		1	.0000	18
	1	.0107	9		2	.0037	13		2	.0004	17
	2	.0547	8		3	.0176	12		3	.0022	16
	3	.1719	7		4	.0592	11		4	.0096	15
	4	.3770	6		5	.1509	10		5	.0318	14
	5	.6230	5		6	.3036	9		6	.0835	13
					7	.5000	8		7	.1796	12
									8	.3238	11
									9	.5000	10

continued

TABLE B
Continued

n	Left S	P	Right S	n	Left S	P	Right S	n	Left S	P	Right S
20	0	.0000	20	20	4	.0059	16	20	8	.2517	12
	1	.0000	19		5	.0207	15		9	.4119	11
	2	.0002	18		6	.0577	14		10	.5881	10
	3	.0013	17		7	.1316	13				

For $n > 20$, the probabilities are found from Table A as follows:

$$Z_R = \frac{S - .5 - .5n}{.5\sqrt{n}} \qquad Z_L = \frac{S + .5 - .5n}{.5\sqrt{n}}$$

Desired	Approximated by
Right-tail probability for S	Right-tail probability for Z_R
Left-tail probability for S	Left-tail probability for Z_L

SOURCE: Adapted from Table 2 of *Tables of the Binomial Distribution* (January 1950 with *Corrigenda* 1952 and 1958), National Bureau of Standards, U.S. Government Printing Office, Washington, D.C.

68

TABLE C
Wilcoxon Signed Rank Distribution

Entries labeled *P* in the table are the cumulative probability from each extreme to the value of the signed rank statistic for the given *n*. Left-tail probabilities are given for *T* ≤ *n*(*n* + 1)/4, and right-tail for *T* ≥ *n*(*n* + 1)/4. *T* is interpreted as either T_+ or T_-.

n	Left T	P	Right T	n	Left T	P	Right T	n	Left T	P	Right T
2	0	.250	3	7	10	.289	18	9	17	.285	28
	1	.500	2		11	.344	17		18	.326	27
3	0	.125	6		12	.406	16		19	.367	26
	1	.250	5		13	.469	15		20	.410	25
	2	.375	4		14	.531	14		21	.455	24
	3	.625	3	8	0	.004	36		22	.500	23
4	0	.062	10		1	.008	35	10	0	.001	55
	1	.125	9		2	.012	34		1	.002	54
	2	.188	8		3	.020	33		2	.003	53
	3	.312	7		4	.027	32		3	.005	52
	4	.438	6		5	.039	31		4	.007	51
	5	.562	5		6	.055	30		5	.010	50
5	0	.031	15		7	.074	29		6	.014	49
	1	.062	14		8	.098	28		7	.019	48
	2	.094	13		9	.125	27		8	.024	47
	3	.156	12		10	.156	26		9	.032	46
	4	.219	11		11	.191	25		10	.042	45
	5	.312	10		12	.230	24		11	.053	44
	6	.406	9		13	.273	23		12	.065	43
	7	.500	8		14	.320	22		13	.080	42
6	0	.016	21		15	.371	21		14	.097	41
	1	.031	20		16	.422	20		15	.116	40
	2	.047	19		17	.473	19		16	.138	39
	3	.078	18		18	.527	18		17	.161	38
	4	.109	17	9	0	.002	45		18	.188	37
	5	.156	16		1	.004	44		19	.216	36
	6	.219	15		2	.006	43		20	.246	35
	7	.281	14		3	.010	42		21	.278	34
	8	.344	13		4	.014	41		22	.312	33
	9	.422	12		5	.020	40		23	.348	32
	10	.500	11		6	.027	39		24	.385	31
7	0	.008	28		7	.037	38		25	.423	30
	1	.016	27		8	.049	37		26	.461	29
	2	.023	26		9	.064	36		27	.500	28
	3	.039	25		10	.082	35				
	4	.055	24		11	.102	34				
	5	.078	23		12	.125	33				
	6	.109	22		13	.150	32				
	7	.148	21		14	.180	31				
	8	.188	20		15	.213	30				
	9	.234	19		16	.248	29				

continued

TABLE C
Continued

n	Left T	P	Right T	n	Left T	P	Right T	n	Left T	P	Right T
11	0	.000	66	12	11	.013	67	13	16	.020	75
	1	.001	65		12	.017	66		17	.024	74
	2	.001	64		13	.021	65		18	.029	73
	3	.002	63		14	.026	64		19	.034	72
	4	.003	62		15	.032	63		20	.040	71
	5	.005	61		16	.039	62		21	.047	70
	6	.007	60		17	.046	61		22	.055	69
	7	.009	59		18	.055	60		23	.064	68
	8	.012	58		19	.065	59		24	.073	67
	9	.016	57		20	.076	58		25	.084	66
	10	.021	56		21	.088	57		26	.095	65
	11	.027	55		22	.102	56		27	.108	64
	12	.034	54		23	.117	55		28	.122	63
	13	.042	53		24	.133	54		29	.137	62
	14	.051	52		25	.151	53		30	.153	61
	15	.062	51		26	.170	52		31	.170	60
	16	.074	50		27	.190	51		32	.188	59
	17	.087	49		28	.212	50		33	.207	58
	18	.103	48		29	.235	49		34	.227	57
	19	.120	47		30	.259	48		35	.249	56
	20	.139	46		31	.285	47		36	.271	55
	21	.160	45		32	.311	46		37	.294	54
	22	.183	44		33	.339	45		38	.318	53
	23	.207	43		34	.367	44		39	.342	52
	24	.232	42		35	.396	43		40	.368	51
	25	.260	41		36	.425	42		41	.393	50
	26	.289	40		37	.455	41		42	.420	49
	27	.319	39		38	.485	40		43	.446	48
	28	.350	38		39	.515	39		44	.473	47
	29	.382	37	13	0	.000	91		45	.500	46
	30	.416	36		1	.000	90	14	0	.000	105
	31	.449	35		2	.000	89		1	.000	104
	32	.483	34		3	.001	88		2	.000	103
	33	.517	33		4	.001	87		3	.000	102
12	0	.000	78		5	.001	86		4	.000	101
	1	.000	77		6	.002	85		5	.001	100
	2	.001	76		7	.002	84		6	.001	99
	3	.001	75		8	.003	83		7	.001	98
	4	.002	74		9	.004	82		8	.002	97
	5	.002	73		10	.005	81		9	.002	96
	6	.003	72		11	.007	80		10	.003	95
	7	.005	71		12	.009	79		11	.003	94
	8	.006	70		13	.011	78		12	.004	93
	9	.008	69		14	.013	77		13	.005	92
	10	.010	68		15	.016	76		14	.007	91

continued

70

TABLE C

Continued

n	Left T	P	Right T	n	Left T	P	Right T	n	Left T	P	Right T
14	15	.008	90	14	48	.404	57	15	28	.036	92
	16	.010	89		49	.428	56		29	.042	91
	17	.012	88		50	.452	55		30	.047	90
	18	.015	87		51	.476	54		31	.053	89
	19	.018	86		52	.500	53		32	.060	88
	20	.021	85	15	0	.000	120		33	.068	87
	21	.025	84		1	.000	119		34	.076	86
	22	.029	83		2	.000	118		35	.084	85
	23	.034	82		3	.000	117		36	.094	84
	24	.039	81		4	.000	116		37	.104	83
	25	.045	80		5	.000	115		38	.115	82
	26	.052	79		6	.000	114		39	.126	81
	27	.059	78		7	.001	113		40	.138	80
	28	.068	77		8	.001	112		41	.151	79
	29	.077	76		9	.001	111		42	.165	78
	30	.086	75		10	.001	110		43	.180	77
	31	.097	74		11	.002	109		44	.195	76
	32	.108	73		12	.002	108		45	.211	75
	33	.121	72		13	.003	107		46	.227	74
	34	.134	71		14	.003	106		47	.244	73
	35	.148	70		15	.004	105		48	.262	72
	36	.163	69		16	.005	104		49	.281	71
	37	.179	68		17	.006	103		50	.300	70
	38	.196	67		18	.008	102		51	.319	69
	39	.213	66		19	.009	101		52	.339	68
	40	.232	65		20	.011	100		53	.360	67
	41	.251	64		21	.013	99		54	.381	66
	42	.271	63		22	.015	98		55	.402	65
	43	.292	62		23	.018	97		56	.423	64
	44	.313	61		24	.021	96		57	.445	63
	45	.335	60		25	.024	95		58	.467	62
	46	.357	59		26	.028	94		59	.489	61
	47	.380	58		27	.032	93		60	.511	60

For $n > 15$, the probabilities are found from Table A as follows:

$$Z_{+,R} = \frac{T_+ - .5 - n(n+1)/4}{\sqrt{n(n+1)(2n+1)/24}} \qquad Z_{-,R} = \frac{T_- - .5 - n(n+1)/4}{\sqrt{n(n+1)(2n+1)/24}}$$

Desired	Approximated by
Right-tail probability for T_+	Right-tail probability for $Z_{+,R}$
Right-tail probability for T_-	Right-tail probability for $Z_{-,R}$

SOURCE: Adapted from F. Wilcoxon, S. K. Katti, and R. A. Wilcox (1973), "Critical values and probability levels for the Wilcoxon rank sum test and the Wilcoxon signed rank test," pp. 171-259 in Institute of Mathematical Statistics, Ed., *Selected Tables in Mathematical Statistics*, Vol. 1, with permission of the American Mathematical Society, Providence, RI.

TABLE D
Mann-Whitney-Wilcoxon Distribution

Entries labeled P in the table are the cumulative probability from each extreme to the value of T_X for the given sample sizes $n_1 \leq n_2$ (n_1 is the size of the X sample). Left-tail probabilities are given for $T_X \leq n_1(N + 1)/2$ and right-tail probabilities for $T_X \geq n_1(N + 1)/2$, where $N = n_1 + n_2$.

$n_1 = 1$

n_2	Left T_X	P	Right T_X
1	1	.500	2
2	1	.333	3
	2	.667	2
3	1	.250	4
	2	.500	3
4	1	.200	5
	2	.400	4
	3	.600	3
5	1	.167	6
	2	.333	5
	3	.500	4
6	1	.143	7
	2	.286	6
	3	.429	5
	4	.571	4
7	1	.125	8
	2	.250	7
	3	.375	6
	4	.500	5
8	1	.111	9
	2	.222	8
	3	.333	7
	4	.444	6
	5	.556	5
9	1	.100	10
	2	.200	9
	3	.300	8
	4	.400	7
	5	.500	6
10	1	.091	11
	2	.182	10
	3	.273	9
	4	.364	8
	5	.455	7
	6	.545	6

$n_1 = 2$

n_2	Left T_X	P	Right T_X
2	3	.167	7
	4	.333	6
	5	.667	5
3	3	.100	9
	4	.200	8
	5	.400	7
	6	.600	6
4	3	.067	11
	4	.133	10
	5	.267	9
	6	.400	8
	7	.600	7
5	3	.048	13
	4	.095	12
	5	.190	11
	6	.286	10
	7	.429	9
	8	.571	8
6	3	.036	15
	4	.071	14
	5	.143	13
	6	.214	12
	7	.321	11
	8	.429	10
	9	.571	9
7	3	.028	17
	4	.056	16
	5	.111	15
	6	.167	14
	7	.250	13
	8	.333	12
	9	.444	11
	10	.556	10

$n_1 = 2$

n_2	Left T_X	P	Right T_X
8	3	.022	19
	4	.044	18
	5	.089	17
	6	.133	16
	7	.200	15
	8	.267	14
	9	.356	13
	10	.444	12
	11	.556	11
9	3	.018	21
	4	.036	20
	5	.073	19
	6	.109	18
	7	.164	17
	8	.218	16
	9	.291	15
	10	.364	14
	11	.455	13
	12	.545	12
10	3	.015	23
	4	.030	22
	5	.061	21
	6	.091	20
	7	.136	19
	8	.182	18
	9	.242	17
	10	.303	16
	11	.379	15
	12	.455	14
	13	.545	13

continued

TABLE D
Continued

n_2	Left T_X	P	Right T_X	n_2	Left T_X	P	Right T_X	n_2	Left T_X	P	Right T_X
	$n_1 = 3$			8	6	.006	30		$n_1 = 4$		
					7	.012	29				
3	6	.050	15		8	.024	28	4	10	.014	26
	7	.100	14		9	.042	27		11	.029	25
	8	.200	13		10	.067	26		12	.057	24
	9	.350	12		11	.097	25		13	.100	23
	10	.500	11		12	.139	24		14	.171	22
4	6	.029	18		13	.188	23		15	.243	21
	7	.057	17		14	.248	22		16	.343	20
	8	.114	16		15	.315	21		17	.443	19
4	9	.200	15		16	.388	20		18	.557	18
	10	.314	14		17	.461	19	5	10	.008	30
	11	.429	13		18	.539	18		11	.016	29
	12	.571	12	9	6	.005	33		12	.032	28
5	6	.018	21		7	.009	32		13	.056	27
	7	.036	20		8	.018	31		14	.095	26
	8	.071	19		9	.032	30		15	.143	25
	9	.125	18		10	.050	29		16	.206	24
	10	.196	17		11	.073	28		17	.278	23
	11	.286	16		12	.105	27		18	.365	22
	12	.393	15		13	.141	26		19	.452	21
	13	.500	14		14	.186	25		20	.548	20
6	6	.012	24		15	.241	24	6	10	.005	34
	7	.024	23		16	.300	23		11	.010	33
	8	.048	22		17	.364	22		12	.019	32
	9	.083	21		18	.432	21		13	.033	31
	10	.131	20		19	.500	20		14	.057	30
	11	.190	19	10	6	.003	36		15	.086	29
	12	.274	18		7	.007	35		16	.129	28
	13	.357	17		8	.014	34		17	.176	27
	14	.452	16		9	.024	33		18	.238	26
	15	.548	15		10	.038	32		19	.305	25
7	6	.008	27		11	.056	31		20	.381	24
	7	.017	26		12	.080	30		21	.457	23
	8	.033	25		13	.108	29		22	.543	22
	9	.058	24		14	.143	28	7	10	.003	38
	10	.092	23		15	.185	27		11	.006	37
	11	.133	22		16	.234	26		12	.012	36
	12	.192	21		17	.287	25		13	.021	35
	13	.258	20		18	.346	24		14	.036	34
	14	.333	19		19	.406	23		15	.055	33
	15	.417	18		20	.469	22				
	16	.500	17		21	.531	21				

continued

TABLE D
Continued

n_2	Left T_X	P	Right T_X	n_2	Left T_X	P	Right T_X	n_2	Left T_X	P	Right T_X
	$n_1 = 4$			9	24	.302	32	6	15	.002	45
					25	.355	31		16	.004	44
7	16	.082	32		26	.413	30		17	.009	43
	17	.115	31		27	.470	29		18	.015	42
	18	.158	30		28	.530	28		19	.026	41
	19	.206	29	10	10	.001	50		20	.041	40
	20	.264	28		11	.002	49		21	.063	39
	21	.324	27		12	.004	48		22	.089	38
	22	.394	26		13	.007	47		23	.123	37
	23	.464	25		14	.012	46		24	.165	36
	24	.536	24		15	.018	45		25	.214	35
8	10	.002	42		16	.027	44		26	.268	34
	11	.004	41		17	.038	43		27	.331	33
	12	.008	40		18	.053	42		28	.396	32
	13	.014	39		19	.071	41		29	.465	31
	14	.024	38		20	.094	40		30	.535	30
	15	.036	37		21	.120	39	7	15	.001	50
	16	.055	36		22	.152	38		16	.003	49
	17	.077	35		23	.187	37		17	.005	48
	18	.107	34		24	.227	36		18	.009	47
	19	.141	33		25	.270	35		19	.015	46
	20	.184	32		26	.318	34		20	.024	45
	21	.230	31		27	.367	33		21	.037	44
	22	.285	30		28	.420	32		22	.053	43
	23	.341	29		29	.473	31		23	.074	42
	24	.404	28		30	.527	30		24	.101	41
	25	.467	27						25	.134	40
	26	.533	26		$n_1 = 5$				26	.172	39
9	10	.001	46						27	.216	38
	11	.003	45	5	15	.004	40		28	.265	37
	12	.006	44		16	.008	39		29	.319	36
	13	.010	43		17	.016	38		30	.378	35
	14	.017	42		18	.028	37		31	.438	34
	15	.025	41		19	.048	36		32	.500	33
	16	.038	40		20	.075	35	8	15	.001	55
	17	.053	39		21	.111	34		16	.002	54
	18	.074	38		22	.155	33		17	.003	53
	19	.099	37		23	.210	32		18	.005	52
	20	.130	36		24	.274	31		19	.009	51
	21	.165	35		25	.345	30		20	.015	50
	22	.207	34		26	.421	29		21	.023	49
	23	.252	33		27	.500	28		22	.033	48

continued

74

TABLE D
Continued

n_2	Left T_X	P	Right T_X	n_2	Left T_X	P	Right T_X	n_2	Left T_X	P	Right T_X
	$n_1 = 5$			10	20	.006	60	7	21	.001	63
					21	.010	59		22	.001	62
8	23	.047	47		22	.014	58		23	.002	61
	24	.064	46		23	.020	57		24	.004	60
	25	.085	45		24	.028	56		25	.007	59
	26	.111	44		25	.038	55		26	.011	58
	27	.142	43		26	.050	54		27	.017	57
	28	.177	42		27	.065	53		28	.026	56
	29	.218	41		28	.082	52		29	.037	55
	30	.262	40		29	.103	51		30	.051	54
	31	.311	39		30	.127	50		31	.069	53
	32	.362	38		31	.155	49		32	.090	52
	33	.416	37		32	.185	48		33	.117	51
	34	.472	36		33	.220	47		34	.147	50
	35	.528	35		34	.257	46		35	.183	49
9	15	.000	60		35	.297	45		36	.223	48
	16	.001	59		36	.339	44		37	.267	47
	17	.002	58		37	.384	43		38	.314	46
	18	.003	57		38	.430	42		39	.365	45
	19	.006	56		39	.477	41		40	.418	44
	20	.009	55		40	.523	40		41	.473	43
	21	.014	54						42	.527	42
	22	.021	53			$n_1 = 6$			8	21	.000	69
	23	.030	52							22	.001	68
	24	.041	51	6	21	.001	57		23	.001	67
	25	.056	50		22	.002	56		24	.002	66
	26	.073	49		23	.004	55		25	.004	65
	27	.095	48		24	.008	54		26	.006	64
	28	.120	47		25	.013	53		27	.010	63
	29	.149	46		26	.021	52		28	.015	62
	30	.182	45		27	.032	51		29	.021	61
	31	.219	44		28	.047	50		30	.030	60
	32	.259	43		29	.066	49		31	.041	59
	33	.303	42		30	.090	48		32	.054	58
	34	.350	41		31	.120	47		33	.071	57
	35	.399	40		32	.155	46		34	.091	56
	36	.449	39		33	.197	45		35	.114	55
	37	.500	38		34	.242	44		36	.141	54
10	15	.000	65		35	.294	43		37	.172	53
	16	.001	64		36	.350	42		38	.207	52
	17	.001	63		37	.409	41		39	.245	51
	18	.002	62		38	.469	40		40	.286	50
	19	.004	61		39	.531	39					

continued

TABLE D
Continued

n_2	Left T_X	P	Right T_X	n_2	Left T_X	P	Right T_X	n_2	Left T_X	P	Right T_X
	$n_1 = 6$			10	29	.008	73		45	.191	60
					30	.011	72	7	46	.228	59
8	41	.331	49		31	.016	71		47	.267	58
	42	.377	48		32	.021	70		48	.310	57
	43	.426	47		33	.028	69		49	.355	56
	44	.475	46		34	.036	68		50	.402	55
	45	.525	45		35	.047	67		51	.451	54
9	21	.000	75		36	.059	66		52	.500	53
	22	.000	74		37	.074	65	8	28	.000	84
	23	.001	73		38	.090	64		29	.000	83
	24	.001	72		39	.110	63		30	.001	82
	25	.002	71		40	.132	62		31	.001	81
	26	.004	70		41	.157	61		32	.002	80
	27	.006	69		42	.184	60		33	.003	79
	28	.009	68		43	.214	59		34	.005	78
	29	.013	67		44	.246	58		35	.007	77
	30	.018	66		45	.281	57		36	.010	76
	31	.025	65		46	.318	56		37	.014	75
	32	.033	64		47	.356	55		38	.020	74
	33	.044	63		48	.396	54		39	.027	73
	34	.057	62		49	.437	53		40	.036	72
	35	.072	61		50	.479	52		41	.047	71
	36	.091	60		51	.521	51		42	.060	70
	37	.112	59						43	.076	69
	38	.136	58			$n_1 = 7$			44	.095	68
	39	.164	57						45	.116	67
	40	.194	56	7	28	.000	77		46	.140	66
	41	.228	55		29	.001	76		47	.168	65
	42	.264	54		30	.001	75		48	.198	64
	43	.303	53		31	.002	74		49	.232	63
	44	.344	52		32	.003	73		50	.268	62
	45	.388	51		33	.006	72		51	.306	61
	46	.432	50		34	.009	71		52	.347	60
	47	.477	49		35	.013	70		53	.389	59
	48	.523	48		36	.019	69		54	.433	58
10	21	.000	81		37	.027	68		55	.478	57
	22	.000	80		38	.036	67		56	.522	56
	23	.000	79		39	.049	66	9	28	.000	91
	24	.001	78		40	.064	65		29	.000	90
	25	.001	77		41	.082	64		30	.000	89
	26	.002	76		42	.104	63		31	.001	88
	27	.004	75		43	.130	62		32	.001	87
	28	.005	74		44	.159	61		33	.002	86

continued

TABLE D
Continued

n_2	Left T_X	P	Right T_X	n_2	Left T_X	P	Right T_X	n_2	Left T_X	P	Right T_X
	$n_1 = 7$				43	.028	83	8	55	.097	81
				10	44	.035	82		56	.117	80
9	34	.003	85		45	.044	81		57	.139	79
	35	.004	84		46	.054	80		58	.164	78
	36	.006	83		47	.067	79		59	.191	77
	37	.008	82		48	.081	78		60	.221	76
	38	.011	81		49	.097	77		61	.253	75
	39	.016	80		50	.115	76		62	.287	74
	40	.021	79		51	.135	75		63	.323	73
	41	.027	78		52	.157	74		64	.360	72
	42	.036	77		53	.182	73		65	.399	71
	43	.045	76		54	.209	72		66	.439	70
	44	.057	75		55	.237	71		67	.480	69
	45	.071	74		56	.268	70		68	.520	68
	46	.087	73		57	.300	69	9	36	.000	108
	47	.105	72		58	.335	68		37	.000	107
	48	.126	71		59	.370	67		38	.000	106
	49	.150	70		60	.406	66		39	.000	105
	50	.176	69		61	.443	65		40	.000	104
	51	.204	68		62	.481	64		41	.001	103
	52	.235	67		63	.519	63		42	.001	102
	53	.268	66						43	.002	101
	54	.303	65			$n_1 = 8$			44	.003	100
	55	.340	64						45	.004	99
	56	.379	63	8	36	.000	100		46	.006	98
	57	.419	62		37	.000	99		47	.008	97
	58	.459	61		38	.000	98		48	.010	96
	59	.500	60		39	.001	97		49	.014	95
10	28	.000	98		40	.001	96		50	.018	94
	29	.000	97		41	.001	95		51	.023	93
	30	.000	96		42	.002	94		52	.030	92
	31	.000	95		43	.003	93		53	.037	91
	32	.001	94		44	.005	92		54	.046	90
	33	.001	93		45	.007	91		55	.057	89
	34	.002	92		46	.010	90		56	.069	88
	35	.002	91		47	.014	89		57	.084	87
	36	.003	90		48	.019	88		58	.100	86
	37	.005	89		49	.025	87		59	.118	85
	38	.007	88		50	.032	86		60	.138	84
	39	.009	87		51	.041	85		61	.161	83
	40	.012	86		52	.052	84		62	.185	82
	41	.017	85		53	.065	83		63	.212	81
	42	.022	84		54	.080	82				

continued

TABLE D
Continued

n_2	Left T_X	P	Right T_X	n_2	Left T_X	P	Right T_X	n_2	Left T_X	P	Right T_X
	$n_1 = 8$			10	68	.257	84	9	76	.218	95
					69	.286	83		77	.245	94
9	64	.240	80		70	.317	82		78	.273	93
	65	.271	79		71	.348	81		79	.302	92
	66	.303	78		72	.381	80		80	.333	91
	67	.336	77		73	.414	79		81	.365	90
	68	.371	76		74	.448	78		82	.398	89
	69	.407	75		75	.483	77		83	.432	88
	70	.444	74		76	.517	76		84	.466	87
	71	.481	73						85	.500	86
	72	.519	72		$n_1 = 9$			10	45	.000	135
10	36	.000	116						46	.000	134
	37	.000	115	9	45	.000	126		47	.000	133
	38	.000	114		46	.000	125		48	.000	132
	39	.000	113		47	.000	124		49	.000	131
	40	.000	112		48	.000	123		50	.000	130
	41	.000	111		49	.000	122		51	.000	129
	42	.001	110		50	.000	121		52	.000	128
	43	.001	109		51	.001	120		53	.001	127
	44	.002	108		52	.001	119		54	.001	126
	45	.002	107		53	.001	118		55	.001	125
	46	.003	106		54	.002	117		56	.002	124
	47	.004	105		55	.003	116		57	.003	123
	48	.006	104		56	.004	115		58	.004	122
	49	.008	103		57	.005	114		59	.005	121
	50	.010	102		58	.007	113		60	.007	120
	51	.013	101		59	.009	112		61	.009	119
	52	.017	100		60	.012	111		62	.011	118
	53	.022	99		61	.016	110		63	.014	117
	54	.027	98		62	.020	109		64	.017	116
	55	.034	97		63	.025	108		65	.022	115
	56	.042	96		64	.031	107		66	.027	114
	57	.051	95		65	.039	106		67	.033	113
	58	.061	94		66	.047	105		68	.039	112
	59	.073	93		67	.057	104		69	.047	111
	60	.086	92		68	.068	103		70	.056	110
	61	.102	91		69	.081	102		71	.067	109
	62	.118	90		70	.095	101		72	.078	108
	63	.137	89		71	.111	100		73	.091	107
	64	.158	88		72	.129	99		74	.106	106
	65	.180	87		73	.149	98		75	.121	105
	66	.204	86		74	.170	97		76	.139	104
	67	.230	85		75	.193	96		77	.158	103

continued

TABLE D
Continued

n_2	Left T_X	P	Right T_X	n_2	Left T_X	P	Right T_X	n_2	Left T_X	P	Right T_X
	$n_1 = 9$			60	.000	150		83	.053	127	
				61	.000	149		84	.062	126	
10	78	.178	102	62	.000	148		85	.072	125	
	79	.200	101	63	.000	147		86	.083	124	
	80	.223	100	64	.001	146		87	.095	123	
	81	.248	99	65	.001	145		88	.109	122	
	82	.274	98	66	.001	144		89	.124	121	
	83	.302	97	67	.001	143		90	.140	120	
	84	.330	96	68	.002	142		91	.157	119	
	85	.360	95	69	.003	141		92	.176	118	
	86	.390	94	70	.003	140		93	.197	117	
	87	.421	93	71	.004	139		94	.218	116	
	88	.452	92	72	.006	138		95	.241	115	
	89	.484	91	73	.007	137		96	.264	114	
	90	.516	90	74	.009	136		97	.289	113	
				75	.012	135		98	.315	112	
	$n_1 = 10$			76	.014	134		99	.342	111	
				77	.018	133		100	.370	110	
10	55	.000	155	78	.022	132		101	.398	109	
	56	.000	154	79	.026	131		102	.427	108	
	57	.000	153	80	.032	130		103	.456	107	
	58	.000	152	81	.038	129		104	.485	106	
	59	.000	151	82	.045	128		105	.515	105	

For m or n larger than 10, the probabilities are found from Table A as follows:

$$Z_{X,L} = \frac{T_X + .5 - n_1(N+1)/2}{\sqrt{n_1 n_2 (N+1)/12}} \qquad Z_{X,R} = \frac{T_X - .5 - n_1(N+1)/2}{\sqrt{n_1 n_2 (N+1)/12}}$$

Desired	Approximated by
Left-tail probability for T_X	Left-tail probability for $Z_{X,L}$
Right-tail probability for T_X	Right-tail probability for $Z_{X,R}$

SOURCE: Adapted from F. Wilcoxon, S. K. Katti, and R. A. Wilcox (1973), "Critical values and probability levels for the Wilcoxon rank sum test and the Wilcoxon signed rank test," pp. 171-259 in Institute of Mathematical Statistics, Ed., *Selected Tables in Mathematical Statistics*, Vol. 1, with permission of the American Mathematical Society, Providence, RI.

TABLE E
Chi-Square Distribution

Table entries on all df lines are the values of a chi-square random variable for which the right-tail probability is as given on the top row.

df	.99	.98	.95	.90	.80	.70	.50	.30	.20	.10	.05	.02	.01	.001
1	.00016	.00063	.0039	.016	.064	.15	.46	1.07	1.64	2.71	3.84	5.41	6.64	10.83
2	.02	.04	.10	.21	.45	.71	1.39	2.41	3.22	4.60	5.99	7.82	9.21	13.82
3	.12	.18	.35	.58	1.00	1.42	2.37	3.66	4.64	6.25	7.82	9.84	11.34	16.27
4	.30	.43	.71	1.06	1.65	2.20	3.36	4.88	5.99	7.78	9.49	11.67	13.28	18.46
5	.55	.75	1.14	1.61	2.34	3.00	4.35	6.06	7.29	9.24	11.07	13.39	15.09	20.52
6	.87	1.13	1.64	2.20	3.07	3.83	5.35	7.23	8.56	10.64	12.59	15.03	16.81	22.46
7	1.24	1.56	2.17	2.83	3.82	4.67	6.35	8.38	9.80	12.02	14.07	16.62	18.48	24.32
8	1.65	2.03	2.73	3.49	4.59	5.53	7.34	9.52	11.03	13.36	15.51	18.17	20.09	26.12
9	2.09	2.53	3.32	4.17	5.38	6.39	8.34	10.66	12.24	14.68	16.92	19.68	21.67	27.88
10	2.56	3.06	3.94	4.86	6.18	7.27	9.34	11.78	13.44	15.99	18.31	21.16	23.21	29.59
11	3.05	3.61	4.58	5.58	6.99	8.15	10.34	12.90	14.63	17.28	19.68	22.62	24.72	31.26
12	3.57	4.18	5.23	6.30	7.81	9.03	11.34	14.01	15.81	18.55	21.03	24.05	26.22	32.91
13	4.11	4.76	5.89	7.04	8.63	9.93	12.34	15.12	16.98	19.81	22.36	25.47	27.69	34.53
14	4.66	5.37	6.57	7.79	9.47	10.82	13.34	16.22	18.15	21.06	23.68	26.87	29.14	36.12
15	5.23	5.98	7.26	8.55	10.31	11.72	14.34	17.32	19.31	22.31	25.00	28.26	30.58	37.70
16	5.81	6.61	7.96	9.31	11.15	12.62	15.34	18.42	20.46	23.54	26.30	29.63	32.00	39.29
17	6.41	7.26	8.67	10.08	12.00	13.53	16.34	19.51	21.62	24.77	27.59	31.00	33.41	40.75

Right-Tail Probability

continued

TABLE E
Continued

df	.99	.98	.95	.90	.80	.70	Right-Tail Probability .50	.30	.20	.10	.05	.02	.01	.001
18	7.02	7.91	9.39	10.86	12.86	14.44	17.34	20.60	22.76	25.99	28.87	32.35	34.80	42.31
19	7.63	8.57	10.12	11.65	13.72	15.35	18.34	21.69	23.90	27.20	30.14	33.69	36.19	43.82
20	8.26	9.24	10.85	12.44	14.58	16.27	19.34	22.78	25.04	28.41	31.41	35.02	37.57	45.32
21	8.90	9.92	11.59	13.24	15.44	17.18	20.34	23.86	26.17	29.62	32.67	36.34	38.93	46.80
22	9.54	10.60	12.34	14.04	16.31	18.10	21.34	24.94	27.30	30.81	33.92	37.66	40.29	48.27
23	10.20	11.29	13.09	14.85	17.19	19.02	22.34	26.02	28.43	32.01	35.17	38.97	41.64	49.73
24	10.86	11.99	13.85	15.66	18.06	19.94	23.34	27.10	29.55	33.20	36.42	40.27	42.98	51.18
25	11.52	12.70	14.61	16.47	18.94	20.87	24.34	28.17	30.68	34.38	37.65	41.57	44.31	52.62
26	12.20	13.41	15.38	17.29	19.82	21.79	25.34	29.25	31.80	35.56	38.88	42.86	45.64	54.05
27	12.88	14.12	16.15	18.11	20.70	22.72	26.34	30.32	32.91	36.74	40.11	44.14	46.96	55.48
28	13.56	14.85	16.93	18.94	21.59	23.65	27.34	31.39	34.03	37.92	41.34	45.42	48.28	56.89
29	14.26	15.57	17.71	19.77	22.48	24.58	28.34	32.46	35.14	39.09	42.56	46.69	49.59	58.30
30	14.95	16.31	18.49	20.60	23.36	25.51	29.34	33.53	36.25	40.26	43.77	47.96	50.89	59.70

For df > 30, the probabilities based on the asymptotic distribution are approximated as follows:
Let Q be a chi-square random variable with degrees of freedom df. A right- or left-tail probability for Q is approximated by a right- or left-tail probability, respectively, from Table A for Z, where

$$Z = \sqrt{2Q} - \sqrt{2(df)} - 1$$

SOURCE: Adapted from Table IV of R. A. Fisher and F. Yates (1963), *Statistical Tables for Biological, Agricultural and Medical Research*, Hafner Publishing Company, New York, with permission of Longman Group Ltd., United Kingdom.

TABLE F
Kruskal-Wallis Distribution

Each table entry is the smallest value of the Kruskal-Wallis Q such that its right-tail probability is less than or equal to the value given on the top row for $k = 3$, each sample size less than or equal to five.

	Right-tail probability for Q				
n_1, n_2, n_3	0.100	0.050	0.020	0.010	0.001
2, 2, 2	4.571	—	—	—	—
3, 2, 1	4.286	—	—	—	—
3, 2, 2	4.500	4.714	—	—	—
3, 3, 1	4.571	5.143	—	—	—
3, 3, 2	4.556	5.361	6.250	—	—
3, 3, 3	4.622	5.600	6.489	7.200	—
4, 2, 1	4.500	—	—	—	—
4, 2, 2	4.458	5.333	6.000	—	—
4, 3, 1	4.056	5.208	—	—	—
4, 3, 2	4.511	5.444	6.144	6.444	—
4, 3, 3	4.709	5.791	6.564	6.745	—
4, 4, 1	4.167	4.967	6.667	6.667	—
4, 4, 2	4.555	5.455	6.600	7.036	—
4, 4, 3	4.545	5.598	6.712	7.144	8.909
4, 4, 4	4.654	5.692	6.962	7.654	9.269
5, 2, 1	4.200	5.000	—	—	—
5, 2, 2	4.373	5.160	6.000	6.533	—
5, 3, 1	4.018	4.960	6.044	—	—
5, 3, 2	4.651	5.251	6.124	6.909	—
5, 3, 3	4.533	5.648	6.533	7.079	8.727
5, 4, 1	3.987	4.985	6.431	6.955	—
5, 4, 2	4.541	5.273	6.505	7.205	8.591
5, 4, 3	4.549	5.656	6.676	7.445	8.795
5, 4, 4	4.668	5.657	6.953	7.760	9.168
5, 5, 1	4.109	5.127	6.145	7.309	—
5, 5, 2	4.623	5.338	6.446	7.338	8.938
5, 5, 3	4.545	5.705	6.866	7.578	9.284
5, 5, 4	4.523	5.666	7.000	7.823	9.606
5, 5, 5	4.560	5.780	7.220	8.000	9.920

For $k > 3$, right-tail probabilities for Q are found from Table E with $k - 1$ degrees of freedom.

SOURCE: Adapted from R. L. Iman, D. Quade, and D. A. Alexander (1975), "Exact probability levels for the Kruskal-Wallis test," pp. 329-384 in Institute of Mathematical Statistics, Ed., *Selected Tables in Mathematical Statistics,* Vol. 3, with permission of the American Mathematical Society, Providence, RI.

TABLE G
Friedman's S Distribution

Entries labeled P in the table are the cumulative probability, right-tail from the value of S to its maximum value, for all $P \leq .50$, $B \leq 8$ for $T = 3$, $B \leq 4$ for $T = 4$.

T	B	S	P	T	B	S	P	T	B	S	P
3	2	8	.167	3	7	54	.021	4	3	35	.054
		6	.500			50	.027			33	.075
	3	18	.028			42	.051			29	.148
		14	.194			38	.085			27	.175
		8	.361			32	.112			25	.207
	4	32	.005			26	.192			21	.300
		26	.042			24	.237			19	.342
		24	.069			18	.305			17	.446
		18	.125			14	.486	4	4	80	.000
		14	.273		8	128	.000			78	.001
		8	.431			126	.000			76	.001
	5	50	.001			122	.000			74	.001
		42	.008			114	.000			72	.002
		38	.024			104	.000			70	.003
		32	.039			98	.001			68	.003
		26	.093			96	.001			66	.006
		24	.124			86	.002			64	.007
		18	.182			78	.005			62	.012
		14	.367			74	.008			58	.014
	6	72	.000			72	.010			56	.019
		62	.002			62	.018			54	.033
		56	.006			56	.030			52	.036
		54	.008			54	.038			50	.052
		50	.012			50	.047			48	.054
		42	.029			42	.079			46	.068
		38	.052			38	.120			44	.077
		32	.072			32	.149			42	.094
		26	.142			26	.236			40	.105
		24	.184			24	.285			38	.141
		18	.252			18	.355			36	.158
		14	.430	4	2	20	.042			34	.190
	7	98	.000			18	.167			32	.200
		96	.000			16	.208			30	.242
		86	.000			14	.375			26	.324
		78	.001			12	.458			24	.355
		74	.003		3	45	.002			22	.389
		72	.004			43	.002			20	.432
		62	.008			41	.017				
		56	.016			37	.033				

continued

TABLE G
Continued

For T and B outside the range of this table, right-tail probabilities are found from Table E as follows:

$$Q = \frac{12S}{BT(T+1)}$$

Desired	Approximated by
Right-tail probability for S	Right-tail probability for Q with $T - 1$ degrees of freedom

SOURCE: Adapted from Table 5 of M. G. Kendall and J. D. Gibbons (1990), *Rank Correlation Methods*, Edward Arnold, United Kingdom, with permission of Hodder & Stoughton Ltd., United Kingdom.

84

TABLE H
Values of Z_c for Multiple Comparisons

An entry in the table for a given c and level of significance α is the quantile point of the standard normal distribution such that the right-tail probability is equal to $\alpha/2c$. For values of c outside the range of this table, Z can be found from Table A by linear interpolation.

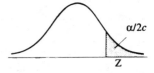

Overall Level of Significance α

c	.30	.25	.20	.15	.10	.05
1	1.036	1.150	1.282	1.440	1.645	1.960
2	1.440	1.534	1.645	1.780	1.960	2.241
3	1.645	1.732	1.834	1.960	2.128	2.394
4	1.780	1.863	1.960	2.080	2.241	2.498
5	1.881	1.960	2.054	2.170	2.326	2.576
6	1.960	2.037	2.128	2.241	2.394	2.638
7	2.026	2.100	2.189	2.300	2.450	2.690
8	2.080	2.154	2.241	2.350	2.498	2.734
9	2.128	2.200	2.287	2.394	2.539	2.773
10	2.170	2.241	2.326	2.432	2.576	2.807
11	2.208	2.278	2.362	2.467	2.608	2.838
12	2.241	2.301	2.394	2.498	2.638	2.866
15	2.326	2.394	2.475	2.576	2.713	2.935
21	2.450	2.515	2.593	2.690	2.823	3.038
28	2.552	2.615	2.690	2.785	2.913	3.125

SOURCE: Adapted from Table IX of R. A. Fisher and F. A. Yates (1963), *Statistical Tables for Biological, Agricultural and Medical Research*, Hafner Publishing Company, New York, with permission of Longman Group Ltd., United Kingdom.

APPENDIX B: FURTHER READING

BRADLEY, J. V. (1968) Distribution-Free Statistical Tests. Englewood Cliffs, NJ: Prentice-Hall.

CONOVER, W. J. (1980) Practical Nonparametric Statistics. New York: John Wiley.

DANIEL, W. (1990) Applied Nonparametric Statistics. Boston: PWS-Kent.

GIBBONS, J. D. (1985) Nonparametric Methods for Quantitative Analysis (2nd ed.). Syracuse, NY: American Sciences Press.

GIBBONS, J. D. (1992) Nonparametric Measures of Association. Newbury Park, CA: Sage.

GIBBONS, J. D., and CHAKRABORTI, S. (1992) Nonparametric Statistical Inference (3rd ed.). New York: Marcel Dekker.

KENDALL, M. G., and GIBBONS, J. D. (1990) Rank Correlation Methods (5th ed.). New York: Oxford University Press.

LEACH, C. (1979) Introduction to Statistics: A Nonparametric Approach for the Social Sciences. New York: John Wiley.

MARASCUILO, L. A., and McSWEENEY, M. (1977) Nonparametric and Distribution-Free Methods for the Social Sciences. Monterey, CA: Brooks/Cole.

SIEGEL, S., and CASTELLAN, N. J. (1988) Nonparametric Statistics for the Behavioral Sciences (2nd ed.). New York: McGraw-Hill.

REFERENCES

BOROD, J. C., CARON, H. S., and KOFF, E. (1984) "Left-handers and right-handers compared on performance and preference measures of lateral dominance." British Journal of Psychology 75: 177-186.

COVINGTON, M. V., and OMELICH, C. L. (1987) "I knew it cold before the exam: A test of the anxiety-blockage hypothesis." Journal of Educational Psychology 79: 393-400.

FOURQURCAN, J. M. (1987) "A K-ABC and WISC-R comparison for Latino learning-disabled children of limited English proficiency." Journal of School Psychology 25: 15-21.

FOWLER, J. F. (1983) "Use of computer-assisted instruction in introductory management science." Journal of Experimental Education 52: 22-26.

GIBBONS, J. D. (1992) Nonparametric Measures of Association. Newbury Park, CA: Sage.

HARTLEY, L. R. (1973) "Effect of prior noise or prior performance on serial reaction." Journal of Experimental Psychology 101: 255-261.

McCABE, A. E. (1987) "Failure in class-inclusion reasoning in a university sample." Journal of Psychology 121: 351-357.

PHILIPS, H. C. (1985) "Return of fear in the treatment of a fear of vomiting." Behavioral Research Therapy 23: 45-52.

SHEARER, L. (1982) "Pierpoint's presidential report card." Parade Magazine (January 7).

TAYLOR, R. L., ZIEGLER, E. W., and PARTENIO, I. (1984) "An investigation of WISC-R verbal-performance differences as a function of ethnic group." Psychology in the Schools 21: 437-445.

WILLIAMS, P. B., and CARNINE, D. W. (1981) "Relationship between range of examples and of instructions and attention in concept attainment." Journal of Educational Research 74: 144-146.

ABOUT THE AUTHOR

JEAN DICKINSON GIBBONS is the Thomas D. Russell Professor of Applied Statistics at the University of Alabama. She earned the Ph.D. degree in statistics from Virginia Polytechnic Institute and State University, after earning the B.A. and M.A. degrees in mathematics from Duke University. She was an Associate Professor of Statistics at the Wharton School of the University of Pennsylvania before taking her present position. She has published several books on nonparametric statistics; some of these are theoretical and some are applied. She has also published numerous articles, which have appeared in the *Journal of the American Statistical Association, American Statistician, Journal of the Royal Statistical Society,* and the *Journal of Quality Technology,* among others. She has been a Fellow of the American Statistical Association since 1972 and has been elected to that organization's Board of Directors for four different terms. She has also been active in consulting and contract teaching in nonparametric statistics for the U.S. Army Logistics Management College of the Department of Defense.

Quantitative Applications in the Social Sciences

A SAGE UNIVERSITY PAPERS SERIES

$9.95 each

SAGE PUBLICATIONS, INC.
P.O. BOX 5084
THOUSAND OAKS, CALIFORNIA 91359-9924

Place
Stamp
here